# The La Dolce Vita Formula

## A Woman's Guide to a Fearless and Fabulous Life

by Heather Picken

**Disclaimer**

This book is provided for personal and informational purposes only. The health-related information provided in this book is not a substitute for a face-to-face consultation with your physician, and should not be interpreted as individual medical advice. If a health condition persists, please contact your physician. This book is not to be interpreted as any attempt to either prescribe or practice medicine. Nor is the book to be understood as putting forth any cure for any type of acute or chronic health problem. Always consult a competent, fully licensed medical professional when making any decision about your health.

The publishers of this book will use reasonable efforts to include up-to-date and accurate information in this book, but make no representations, warranties, or assurances as to the accuracy, currency, or completeness of the information provided. The owners of this book shall not be liable for any damages or injury resulting from your access to, or inability to access, this book, or from your reliance on any information provided in this book.

# TABLE OF CONTENTS

**READ THIS FIRST!**

Go to

**www.FearlessandFabulousVision.com**

to download your FREE La Dolce Vita Vision worksheet. You'll need it to complete the exercise in Chapter 6.

You can also visit **www.HeatherPicken.com** to get access to free trainings, articles, and the author's show.

To Ed
Thanks for supporting me with my vision, mission, and purpose.
You inspire me to live my La Dolce Vita Life!

**"Be who you are and blaze your own trail of uniqueness"**

# INTRODUCTION

Are you truly fulfilled in your life? Do you feel empty, like there's something missing? Have you tried to set goals, only to be beaten back because there was always something or someone that got in your way? Do you know, deep inside, that you are capable of having so much more in your life, but feel frustrated because you are blocked? Maybe you want to make more money in your business or advance further in your career. Perhaps one of your goals is to get in better shape, but each time you try you fall back into the same old patterns and habits that keep you stuck in place. Or is your life falling apart because you're not letting go of a bad relationship? Or are you in between relationships, fearful of putting yourself out there to start dating again?

Whatever your story, if you're reading this, you're an ambitious woman who wants more and is not about to give up on herself. You just need coaching to learn how to break through whatever is blocking you so you can be free to pursue your dreams. *The La Dolce Vita Formula: A Woman's Guide to a Fearless and Fabulous Life* is all about helping you shatter your limitations so you can create the life you want.

I wrote this book specifically for you because I've been disempowered in every area of my own life, from money to men, and it's my mission to help women just like you. I came up with the concept for *The La Dolce Vita Formula* back when I was living in Florence, Italy. Studying Italian culture and seeing how the Italian people lived—working hard but enjoying all that life has to offer—inspired me to take a hard look at why, exactly, I felt "stuck" in my own life. I asked myself, *Why can't I find my own formula for living that makes me feel fulfilled?*

In *The La Dolce Vita Formula*, I will share my discoveries with you so you can uncover your personal unique formula for a successful life. You'll learn how to get crystal clear on setting goals and going after your true desires. But you'll also learn the crucial skill of how to get out of your own way. By the end of this program, you'll know how to live a fulfilling life on your own terms, and no longer will you settle for anything less. I will also show you how to reprogram your mindset for success so that you create habits that stick, habits that propel you forward. And you'll be inspired, as I am, by the stories I share of powerful Italian women who blazed their own trails, staying true to themselves and changing history.

By the end of this book, you'll realize that no matter what's happened to you in the past, your destiny is to live an inspired life.

### Growing Up with Challenges

At four years old, I saw myself as this cute little blonde girl with pigtails, but I had trouble walking and had to wear metal braces for a few years. I didn't think much about what was strapped to my legs. I knew I was different, but didn't feel there was anything really wrong with me. I remember looking at a picture of myself at the petting zoo in Erie, PA, eating an ice cream cone, wearing a pink shirt and plaid shorts. My metal braces were strapped my legs as if I was some kind of robot, but I was happy in my own little world.

It wasn't until I was in fourth grade that I began to believe there was something wrong with me. Reading and writing were major challenges. I was often taken out of my classroom in front of my peers and escorted to the room next door. That room was all glass windows, and as I sat at the big, long, wooden table, facing toward my classmates, I thought to myself, *What's wrong with me? Why am I in this room? Why is this person who is sitting across from me asking me to draw circles?* These were questions I didn't bother to ask out loud, so I never received answers. Instead, I created a label for myself: "stupid." This was my first self-limiting belief.

While my peers excelled at their classwork, I was locked in a holding pattern. It took me an hour to read one page, and I still couldn't comprehend what I had read. During class my mind constantly wandered. At first my parents thought I was goofing off in school, since I was bringing home D's and F's. In reality, my brain was wired differently. And they didn't even have a word for it, or at least if they did no one sat me down to tell it to me. Nor did they say, "Heather, there's nothing wrong with you, we just need to work on your skills a bit more." It wasn't until later that they finally diagnosed me as dyslexic.

I didn't care for school that much as I got older and my academic struggles continued. It took me hours to study for tests just to land a C, while my sister with a photographic memory would nail her tests with straight A's. I can recall comparing myself to her and reinforcing my self-applied label of being stupid. This belief grew stronger as I kept encountering setbacks. I desperately wanted something in my life that would help me feel good about myself.

High school was better, as I started to learn more about myself and to own my power. I discovered my love for fashion. However, my health suffered because my constant comparing of my body to those of other girls led me to develop an eating disorder, anorexia.

I was super thin, my hair was drying up, and my skin was turning yellow. Thankfully, I got wise and realized this wasn't a healthy mindset. I was able to rehabilitate myself by learning about the dangers of anorexia. Looking back, I realize now that this was the first time I used my own smarts, intuition, and discipline to overcome a self-destructive habit.

I still struggled with my grades during high school—since my focus was on boys and being popular and fashionable—and barely graduated with a C-. Since I had a love for fashion and aspired to be the next Armani fashion designer, I applied for the Fashion Design School at Kent State. But I was heartbroken when they rejected me, and remember asking my mom, "What's wrong with me? This is my dream. Why am I so stupid?" At least I was accepted into the regular college program at Kent State, but now that studying fashion wasn't an option I was uninterested in learning. However, my parents insisted I go to college and get an education. I spent some time just taking electives, but I had to drop out of just about every class because I couldn't comprehend physics or astronomy. They all had math components, and since I had dyslexia I was terrible with numbers. I remember thinking at the time that I wanted to drop out of college altogether and dismiss myself from life. Through it all, I kept asking myself the question: *What do I really want to do with my life?*

Then one day my interest was piqued when I noticed some posters describing the art classes offered by the school. I thought to myself, *I could do this. This sounds like fun!* My mind brimming with enthusiasm and possibilities, that same day I declared my major for a BFA (bachelor of fine arts) with a concentration in film. The first day of film class changed my life, as I sat in the classroom (which was converted into a dark theater), learning from my hip professor, Cindy Penter. She was an eccentric woman with jet-black hair who had a love of light, film, and feminine studies. I loved film. It was a world where I could escape and express myself, especially during my darkest times. It allowed me to unleash my creativity and not feel like I was being judged. Soon I took a crack at making my first film, and for the first time in my life I felt excited, creative, and alive. That semester I made the Dean's list, a remarkable academic turnaround. I was a female Spike Lee in the making! Finally, I had discovered what I loved and I was damn good at it.

One day, Professor Penter showed the class a film by the Italian filmmaker Federico Fellini (imagine saying that name in your best Italian voice). The film was *La Dolce Vita*, which means "The Sweet Life." This mysterious black and white film mesmerized me with its subtleties and storyline, and I enjoyed trying to dissect its meaning and learning from a master filmmaker moviemaking's formulas and terminology. I was fascinated, and it didn't matter that I didn't know half the movie's meaning. A few months later, I found out about an international program where I could study and live in Florence, Italy. I was so excited I shared the news with my film buddies, Johnnie and Ben. I told them about the program and said, "I've decided I will be moving to Italy!" When they asked me how I could be so sure that I was going, I replied that I was so certain it would happen that I didn't have any doubt. The next thing you know, I was on a plane to Florence. I didn't realize it at the time, but I was embarking on an adventure that would be a turning point in my life.

When I got there, I told myself I wanted to learn from the greatest artists and philosophers Italy had to offer, people like Leonardo Di Vinci. During that time living abroad, I consciously took in everything I could. Studying Italian culture and absorbing the daily life of the Italian people gave me a new perspective on health, happiness, and wealth, and I came to appreciate their way of living embodied by the phrase *la dolce vita* (just like the name of the movie that inspired me). It made me realize that back home I had been "playing small." Now I felt eager to step up my game. In Italy, I developed my own technique of observing people by sitting at the local cafés for hours while drinking cappuccinos and perfecting my Italian accent. I fit in so well people thought I was Italian! And I felt the same way because I *believed* it, even if it was for only a brief moment in time. I had an Italian boyfriend who owned a *gelatoria*. My days consisted of him picking me on his Vespa and riding recklessly down the narrow cobblestone streets of Florence.

Life in Italy was wonderful, but when I got back to the States I lost my *la dolce vita* swagger. As time passed, I kept attracting bad relationships. It seemed the more I forced things the worse they became. I would break up from one relationship and attract another guy, only to endure learning life's next lesson. At the same time my love life was a mess, so was my money situation. I became unraveled from all of my stress and began to gain weight. I didn't have the perspective at the time to realize that all of these struggles were creating something valuable deep inside me—an understanding of my authentic inner self and of my true personal values—that would come to serve me well in life. Thankfully, I was able to take the lessons I learned from these challenges and turn them into blessings. The hard times taught me to persevere, be patient with myself, and keep going, even when I felt like I wanted to stop. Gradually, I started to develop a formula for life that help me deal with all the obstacles that no one ever gave me the guidebook on.

I've shared my story with you because I've learned the hard way how to overcome being disempowered. Today I love my life, am having fun being my true self, and have finally figured out the formula for living fabulously. I've made it my mission to empower millions of women to use my La Dolce Vita Formula program to master every area of their life so they, too, can overcome their problems and live the fulfilling life they deserve.

### The La Dolce Vita Formula

The La Dolce Vita Formula, inspired by the Italian people's zest for life, is different for every single person on this planet. But once you use this book to discover your unique, personal formula, you'll *never* go back to your old ways of negative thinking and being. You will stay true to who you are because you'll be setting and achieving goals that are in alignment with your deepest values. And here's the exciting part! The more you do this, the bigger the ambitions you will set for yourself because no longer will you be trying to live your life for others or beating yourself up over unmet goals. You will finally understand who you really are and why you're here. The challenges you face will be easily surpassed or not even perceived as challenges in the first place, because you will be empowered by a new way of thinking and being.

> *"Once you discover your unique, personal formula, you'll never go back to your old ways of negative thinking and being."*

*The La Dolce Vita Formula: A Woman's Guide To a Fearless and Fabulous Life* is for you if you've been struggling to accomplish your dreams and goals. This book contains secrets to living the sweet life that could be the missing puzzle pieces you have been looking for! These secrets, combined with state-of-the-art insights about psychology, mindset, and motivation, are packaged into a step-by-step guide designed for *you*, the modern, ambitious woman who wants to live and play full-out.

As you work your way through the book, I will teach you the eight steps that comprise the La Dolce Vita Formula, and I'll guide you through a series of exercises that will reveal you own personal recipe for living a fabulous and fulfilling life. A perfect blend of science, psychology, and philosophy with a modern twist, *The La*

*Dolce Vita Formula* will first focus on getting you crystal clear about who you are and what you *really* want. Then, as we further develop the formula, you'll be able to identify what roadblocks are getting in your way and preventing you from making more money, starting a new adventure, attracting a better relationship, creating your ideal body, or getting clear on your life's purpose. I'll teach you valuable techniques to break through these limitations so you can stay on track.

Now is the time to stop settling and start owning your power! It's time to go after your desires so that you create a rich and wonderful life. Most women give up who they are and detour away from their dreams. Sometimes they stop because they are fearful of what people might say. Does this perhaps describe you? Are you afraid of failing? Are you afraid of looking stupid?

When you don't follow your truth, you create resentment for both yourself and the people around you. This result in a reduced existence for you, and eats away at your happiness Each time you criticize yourself, you minimize yourself. Your self-worth decreases and your doubt increases. Trust me, I know this to be true because I went through it all myself.

Are you failing to achieve your goals because you're all over the place and you can't seem to take action and follow through? As a result, do you give yourself excuses about being overwhelmed or about there not being enough time? Are you unable to figure out *why* your life is not harmoniously flowing toward the goals you want to accomplish, and are you therefore feeling a deep void? Do you tell yourself you're a failure, the way I told myself I was stupid when I was a struggling child? You might even wonder if there's something wrong with you, like I did.

The truth is . . . there is *nothing* wrong with you. You just haven't yet discovered your unique formula for living a fulfilling life. And no one has bothered to show you.

Let's fix that situation! You have a hidden, fingerprint-specific formula that is just waiting to be unleashed, a formula that can make your life flow. This book will help you find and follow this formula, and when you do, the stars will seem to align and doors will open effortlessly for you. If you come to understand that everything is *energy*, and what you put out the Universe sends back times 100, then you will never want to stop following your destiny. You only need to give yourself *permission* to follow your deepest desires.

Here's to living your La Dolce Vita Life!

—Heather

# Part One
# How to Find Your Life's Purpose

**"Knowing who you are, your true self... is like having a Super Power"**

# CHAPTER ONE
# WHAT ARE VALUES?

*"I'm selfish, impatient, and a little insecure. I make mistakes, I'm out of control, and at times hard to handle. But if you can't handle me at my worst, then you sure as hell don't deserve me at my best." —Marilyn Monroe*

If you're ambitious like me, you might have already set and accomplished a number of goals in your lifetime. You feel proud about what you've done, but you want more. Perhaps you are asking yourself, *Why can't I get to the next level?* You're driven and not about to let this get the best of you, either—but it can be frustrating setting a goal and not being able to reach it. Or being unable to do something at your highest level of potential. I get it! As human beings, we will never be satisfied with living unfulfilled lives. We are wired to keep setting goals and growing to the next level.

When I work with one of my private clients, the very first thing that I do—*before* we map out any goals—is determine her values. Why? Because determining your values is the fastest path to identifying and setting goals you can actually achieve. In other words, your true inner values guide you to your goals. This insight is something that most people aren't aware of, and it certainly isn't taught in school. Most books on goal setting will break the process down into small steps and tell you to have an action plan. For example, you might have heard of the well known SMART (specific, measurable, agreed, relevant, and time-bound) goals system, which describes the essential parts of setting realistic goals.

While setting realistic goals is important, the La Dolce Vita Formula takes you one step further by aligning your values, your inner sense of what's important to your life, with the *right* goals, the ones that will bring true success and fulfillment. By following this values-driven formula—which will be revealed in this book as you go through the chapters and exercises—you'll be able to set goals that, when met, will bring to you deep satisfaction, while at the same time make you hungry to do more.

The origins of the formula in this book (and why it starts off by talking about values) can be traced back to the ancient Greeks. They created a field of study called teleology, which is the study of the highest purpose and meaning for a human being. The Greeks also talked about living from the *telos*, which they referred to as a person's inner mechanism that is the catalyst for pursuing one's life-purpose. Your *telos* is like your brain's internal GPS: it will always lead you down the path you need to go. Once you use the La Dolce Vita Formula to make yourself sensitive and attuned to your *telos*—your inner sense of purpose—you'll never let the setbacks that inevitably come along to get in the way of living a fabulous life. You will be supported by having clear goals in mind and a game plan in place that will guide your every step. In fact, if you follow your unique formula, you'll learn to embrace the very challenges that right now might seem daunting to you.

The La Dolce Vita Formula will open your eyes to the magnitude of what you can do. Understand that you are programmed to keep moving forward, that you are destined to live a life that is unique to you, and that there's no stopping what you can do. But to get to where you want to go, it's important to study other successful people who have done the sorts of thing you want to do. You might observe that these people seem to have their own formulas for achievement, and that a big part of their success lies in being able to break through the barriers in their way. They keep going—no matter what. Later in this book, I will share with you some of the powerful methods successful people use to master their mental state and stay on target.

The Greeks also created a field of inquiry called axiology, which is the study of values and worth. They concluded that no two people on the planet have the same set of values; meaning, we all see the world in a different "fingerprint-specific" way because we all have different priorities that we focus on in our lives. Most people think that the word "values" means the same as living with integrity. But integrity is defined more through morals and ethics. You can show yourself the real meaning of values by looking closely at your own life. Your true values are demonstrated by the way you live your life right now on a daily basis; not in what you say, but in what you do. Your *actions* indicate what you really value

For most of us, this leads to the question, "Why can't I do what I really want to do?" Here's the missing ingredient that you must understand: your *desires* are what drive your values. So if you're wanting to make more money, be in a relationship, get in better shape, or make more friends, it's your inner wants and needs that are nudging you to fill this void. Let's say you keep telling yourself it's time to lose those last fifteen pounds, yet you keep sabotaging your efforts. There's a reason why this is happening: what you are telling yourself you want is not actually in alignment with who you are and with your true desires. I will talk about self-sabotage and unconscious motives later in this book, but for right now I want to reiterate that it's not what you say but what you *do* that counts. For example, if you are dating someone new and you start to notice that their actions are incongruent with their words—perhaps they don't call when they say they will— you're observing the same thing as what is going on with the dissatisfying parts of your own life.

It took me almost my entire life to understand this aspect of the formula, but once I did it changed the way I approached goals in my life. That's why I am excited to share what I've learned with you. Know that there's nothing wrong with you, you just need to achieve clarity on who you really are and how you're wired to take action.

Let me take a moment to give credit to one of my mentors, Dr. John Demartini. Dr. Demartini originated the Values Determination process which I am certified in and have since adapted for my own program, as I learned to go deeper into the process of uncovering someone's values and finding out what really makes them tick. This process is helpful in determining who you are, your life's purpose, branding your business, and picking the right, achievable goals to set. I really love doing this work for my clients. It's rewarding to see them make the money they want, get the guy of their dreams, and create their ideal body on their own terms. And I look forward to helping you do the same things, too.

As women, we tend to overthink and complicate things. When you forget about the complications and go back to the basics, you'll realize how you can live more in the flow of life instead of forcing yourself.

### The 7 Key Areas of Your Life

Now that you understand that there's a waiting-to-be-discovered La Dolce Vita Formula that can guide you to be the most fabulous and authentic version of yourself that you can be—living from your *telos*, that GPS which drives your desires—let's talk about your values as they apply to the different areas of your life.

**The areas of your life are broken up into the following seven categories:**

1. Life Purpose
2. Family/Relationship

3. Friends
4. Finances
5. Fitness
6. Mindset
7. Vocation/Career/Business

Scan the list above and think about which of those areas in your life you consistently take action in. It's those areas that indicate where your most important values lie; they're the areas that are most aligned with who you are and what you really want. Let's pretend that you're my client and you told me you wanted to make more money in your business. Before I created the blueprint to get you there, I would need to ask you specific questions to find out the hierarchy of your values. These question would involve determining the areas of your life that you are currently most active in. Again, your values are demonstrated by what you are actually doing in your life right now. It's possible that our assessment might tell us that making more money in business is not, in fact, in alignment with your highest values. Surprised? Don't be. This self-discovery process can uncover things about ourselves that we never realized.

Later in this chapter I will give you the formula for understanding your true values, and how they tie into the seven areas of your life. But before we do that, there are some important things about values that you need to understand. One is that your values can change gradually over time as your life changes. A common example of this is having a baby, which would certainly cause you to focus on the family area of life. Values can also change abruptly if you live through a catastrophic or tragic event. However, our objective right now is for you to know your values as they currently are, and then to live by them. Without this knowledge, you're far more likely to attract things into your life that throw you off your path.

To begin the process of you understanding your values, I want to take you through an exercise that will connect the dots between your past and who you are now, and uncover how your values have shaped your journey through life. This powerful tool will help you to see why you believe what you belief, why you've taken the actions you've taken, and why the outcome of your life is what it currently is, for better or worse. Your La Dolce Vita Formula—the key to understanding who you are—is the sum of your experiences. You gave some of those experiences meaning and labeled them good or bad, according to what you perceived. In reality, nothing is good or bad; we filter life through our own personal values and add those tags in the process.

Using the following table as your guide, go back into your life, starting from the earliest moments you can remember, and catalog major or significant events that you labeled good or bad. Take as much time as you need; this exercise is important.

**Age | Event | What I Perceived | What Happened as a Result**

| Age | Event | Perception | Result |
|---|---|---|---|
| | | | |
| | | | |
| | | | |
| | | | |
| | | | |
| | | | |
| | | | |
| | | | |
| | | | |
| | | | |
| | | | |
| | | | |
| | | | |

## How I Turned My Disorder into Order

You probably found the exercise above to be challenging, perhaps even somewhat painful. It's not as easy task to reconstruct the major events of your life in a disciplined way. And the realizations that result can be profound for some people. On that note, let me tell you a bit more about my past, and how it relates to values.

When I was younger, my dyslexia forced me to find order and meaning in my life. At the same time, my desires pushed me to seek out what I felt was *missing* within my values. I wanted to be smart, sexy, popular, and strong. I wanted to have money. And beyond all that, my dissatisfactions inspired me to do something to help others get out of their own way, find amazing relationships, and have fabulous health and vitality. I wanted to crack the code for understanding how to reprogram my mind for success and then use that knowledge to help others.

I mentioned how your values can change over time; as you read this book, you'll see how my values have done just that. These changes happened because I studied and implemented strategies to improve each area of my life that I was disempowered in. I changed who am I, and as a result my values evolved, too. I want you to consciously connect the dots for your life as well, so you can see how who you are now is different from the person you were five or ten years ago. I believe that knowing and understanding your past are important parts of forming the right mindset, which is the key to success in anything you want to have in life.

As I mentioned before, no one sees the world the same way as you do, or as I do. This is why some couples constantly fight: they have completely different sets of values that largely oppose each other. They fight the same fights over and over again because they're not willing to accept that each person's formula for life is different. What if I told you that when you learn what your values are, as well as those of your partner or other important people in your life, you could have whatever you want? I am laughing to myself right now because I know you might be thinking, *Heather that's kind of manipulative*. But the truth is, we all are living according to our personal values, trying to have people see what we see; and, regrettably, when our values don't match someone else's, we tend to label the other person's values as wrong. That's why it's wise to try to understand the values of the important people in your life—it greatly improves communication.

But first you must know and master your own unique formula. This knowledge gives you the strength and perspective to never give in to other people's unreasonable demands. This is what I call "living your truth," and what the Greeks called living from your *telos*. It's the most important thing you can do to discover what makes you unique and fabulous.

Most people don't achieve this level of self-awareness, and that's why they beat themselves up trying to "pretzel" their life for others. Did a light bulb perhaps just go off in your head? Are you thinking, *That's me! I do this self-twisting act with my family, parents, or friends*. My philosophy about this is simple: Why beat yourself up and twist yourself in knots worrying about what others think of you, when you can start living your own glorious *vita*? You're life is all you have. Do you want to get to your last day on Earth and find yourself wishing that you had been more authentic and had owned your own power? How about becoming the most authentic version of yourself *right now* and getting after your crazy, inspiring dreams? I don't know about you, but I want to push the envelope in life!

Again, my values are not going to be the same as yours, and the stories about my past are, of course, only given to provide examples for you to learn from. For instance, my personal values are now aligned with shifting women's consciousnesses so they can become empowered in every area of their life. Every day I get up and ask myself, "Who can I inspire today?" Of course, like everyone, I have my not-so-good days. But I also have the tools in place to transform my negative emotions into something positive. The key is knowing how to balance your mind in every situation, every step of the way.

It saddens me that many women I know live their lives with regrets. They beat themselves up because they're not advocating for themselves. I've done that, and you probably have, too. But if you're reading this book, you're now ready to be inspired to see how fabulous you can be, without needing the approval of others. You're ready to go live your dreams, and set goals that both scare you and push you to the highest level. Trust me: I'm the perfect person to coach and motivate you along this journey. I'll call you out when you're giving me a story as to why things can't work out. I've been there and I know where you're coming from. I've played the victim in life, and now I'm playing the victor. You will, too.

### Staying True to Your Values Is the Key to Success

How do you succeed in life? By living your values and loving yourself enough to be, do, and have whatever you want. It's time to stop settling. You must embrace being uncomfortable at times. It's in the places of discomfort that you grow the most, because without challenges or challengers (and we all have those sorts of people in our lives), you keep yourself playing it safe and playing small. Give yourself permission to follow your true path. That path is always there to guide you, waiting for you to stay focused and take action on your dreams so you can be the trailblazer of your life.

It's also important to realize that along your journey in life, other people—in the form of your parents, various authority figures, society—have, usually with the best of intentions, been injecting their own values into you. They've told you to live this way or live that way. Well, I'm here to tell you that you need to follow your own values, despite what others may say. Knowing who you are, your true inner self, is like having a superpower. Once you fully embrace a deep knowledge of yourself and your internal driving forces, you stop the second-guessing and start taking action. I want you to get excited because I'm here to assist you in getting what you want.

But I do want to issue a word of caution before we go any further. Because, as we've discussed, each person has their own set of values, it's wise for you to guard and keep your goals and dreams to yourself. Only share them with people who you trust, and who share values similar to yours. And should you express your dreams to somebody who doesn't approve of what you are doing, don't blame them; they are just looking at your goals through the lens of what they value. Understanding this is the secret in not allowing others to steal you away from your dreams, for it is your destiny to live life on your terms, and not seek the approval of others with different viewpoints and agendas.

The Greeks said it best: "Know thyself, love thyself, be thyself." If this is true, you might ask, "Then why do we get distracted from what we say we really want, and then later beat ourselves up because we don't get there?" The answer is simple: when you do not truly know who you are, you will take on other people's identities and try to fit yourself into their way of thinking and being—which is not *you*. That won't happen once you discover your La Dolce Vita Formula.

*"The Italians have their priorities right: They're driven, they do their work, but they really enjoy the day-to-day and they don't put off the enjoyment of the everyday for some future goal." —Frances Mayes*

**Fearless and Fabulous Female Profile**

**Rita Levi-Montalcini** (1909–2012) was born into a Jewish family, where her father was an engineer and her mother a painter. Rita herself studied medicine in Turin. Because of her Jewish heritage, in 1938 she was forced into hiding by Italy's fascist government, so she built a small laboratory in her room and began her experiments to study the nerve fibers in chicken embryos. She worked with her professor, Giuseppe Levi, who also proudly served as her first assistant. At the end of World War II, Rita moved to St. Louis, where she continued her work and made important discoveries in the field of neurobiology. In 1986, Rita Levi-Montalcini was awarded the Nobel Prize in Medicine for her discovery (along with Stanley Cohen) of nerve growth factor.

Because Rita decided to fully dedicate her entire life to science, she made the choice to not marry or start a family. She was an important leader of the Italian feminist movement and a senator of the Italian Parliament. Here are two of her quotes:

"The women had to fight doubly. They always had to carry two burdens, the private one and the social one. Women are the spine of society."

"The woman had been caged for ages. When she finally reached the culture she was ravenous. The food is more useful for who is starving than for who is satiated."

As you can see, Rita overcame obstacles and made difficult decisions to stay true to her values and pursue the life she wanted. What can you learn from Rita? Do you envision ways in which you can walk your own path of being fearless and fabulous? If you are holding back, how can you channel your energy, like Rita did, to align your actions with your values so that you can achieve your goals, despite what anyone else might say? We all have it within us to live fearlessly like Rita, and it doesn't matter what century you live in.

**Fearless and Fabulous Female Profile**

**Sofia Villani Scicolone** (born 1934), popularly known by her screen name Sophia Loren, is a legendary Italian film star. Counted among the most beautiful and talented actresses to have ruled the cinema world, she was a major celebrity from the 1950s through the 1970s. Born to an unwed mother, Sofia had a difficult childhood. Being an illegitimate child meant having no father figure and living in extreme poverty for the first fifteen years of her life. Aptly nicknamed "Little Stick," she was shy, ugly, and lean as a child. Little did she know that one day she would become a sex symbol in the United States and throughout Europe. Her fortune changed when at fifteen she was spotted by a producer (her future husband) in a beauty pageant. From there she went from being an unknown face to a huge movie star, and in no time garnered a tremendous following of admirers. Several prestigious awards, including the Best Actress Oscar, certify that she was not just a pretty face, but a complete and true actress.

As you can see, Sofia's childhood experience of being thought of as ugly created a painful void in her life. She never felt pretty enough. But she was able to take that great negative and use it as the driving force to achieve her highest personal value—being desirable. Regardless of what your own particular challenges may be, you can do something similar. You can be the Sofia Loren of your own life's movie.

My values have certainly changed throughout my life, and yours will, too. I can remember right after college hopping on a plane to New York City (missing my graduation ceremony!) to pursue my career as an independent filmmaker. At that moment in time, that was what my soul was calling me to do. I was fearlessly following my internal GPS without regrets, going against what my family thought was best for me. I was a rebel with long, jet-black hair, ready for adventure. I arrived in New York at night during a huge storm. Looking out the airplane window, the city turned into a giant bowl of electricity. I felt her fire and I started worrying about my choices. *What did I just do? Did I make the right decision? I don't know anyone here, nor have I even seen the place where I am supposed to live.*

Despite my big plans, soon after I arrived I felt a strong disconnect. My values had changed, and I realized that I didn't want to pursue film, and I didn't feel in alignment with living in New York. I was fine with moving back to Ohio, back where one of my voids (which you'll learn about later) drove my highest values.

*"Whatever you perceive is a void in your life will drive your desires."*

## How to Identify Your Values

Identifying your personal values will allow you to set goals that are aligned with who you are. Your goals are much more achievable when they're aligned with your true self. Even when you encounter challenges in fulfilling your goals—such as losing weight, making more money, finding your purpose, or being in an amazing relationship—you will feel that all of the things you want are *on* the way instead of *in* the way. Learning how to master the art of living by your truth opens the door to a truly fabulous and fulfilling life.

Have you ever set a goal that you didn't achieve, and beat yourself up about it afterwards? I can relate because in the past, before I knew my personal La Dolce Vita Formula, I can't tell you how many times I set goals that were completely unrealistic. When I unsurprisingly failed to achieve these goals, I of course assumed there was something wrong with me. As I've mentioned previously, the truth was that there wasn't anything wrong with me; I simply failed to understand that these goals I kept setting were not in alignment with my values. So if you're reading this and nodding your head, then you can relax, because you're about to encounter a proven and predictable science, psychology, and philosophy—an equation for your life—that will ensure that from now on you set goals that you can accomplish.

Earlier I related that when I meet with a new client, I ask them specific questions that give me insight to their fingerprint-specific formula. Once I identify what their true values are, I can help them set goals that are in alignment with those values. It's exciting and rewarding for me to do this because I have the chance make a positive impact on someone's life. Whether I am working with a client privately or they are purchasing my programs, my goal is always the same: to shift their consciousness, be a catalyst, and help them reach the goals they aspire to. I look forward to guiding you through the same process! And it's not all just about *you*. Remember, you are energy and create a vibration with your being.

The more you work on yourself and live your life's purpose, the more it helps and inspires the people around you. If more people thought like this we would see a huge global shift for the better. How you can help is to be the truest expression of yourself, just like in the ancient Greek's philosophy. Stop worrying so much about what you can't control in the world and work on what you can control. Go for your goals in whatever form they may take and you'll inspire others.

By the way, when identifying your personal values, I want you to know that there's nothing wrong with you if your values seem radically different from those of the people around you. Maybe secretly you want to create a lean physique, but you're afraid of what others might think of you. You might even think, *Will I lose my loved ones if I pursue my personal values?* If you have these thoughts (and we all do from time to time), you must ask yourself the question: do I want to live life on my own terms and stay true to myself, or do I want to bow to the wishes of others and, therefore, live a life of resentment?

Now that you have a bit of understanding of what true values are and what they are not (namely values injected into your life by family or society, saying you must be this or do that), you realize that you don't have to take on anyone else's agenda. It's time to focus on *your* agenda, but to do that you must first determine what your personal values are. The exercises in this part of the book will help you do just that.

I am going to ask you specific questions that will reveal your personal values. These values are a key part of your unique formula that differentiates you; no one in the world has precisely the same formula as you. Remember, your personal values are demonstrated by your *current actions* in the different areas of your life. Before we dive in, let me first list again the seven areas of life so that they are fresh in your mind.

1. Life Purpose
2. Family/Relationship
3. Friends
4. Finances
5. Fitness
6. Mindset
7. Vocation/Career/Business

I want you to take a look at your life right now and tell me about something you are passionate about, that occupies most of your mental space. Is there an area in the list above that contains something so inspiring to you that you keep dreaming about it? What actions are you taking, even if they're only small steps?

For example, let's say you've got a goal to make more money in your business, and every day you are taking action on attracting more clients. The actions you're taking might be follow-up phone calls, creating a new marketing strategy to acquire more leads, asking for referrals, etc.

Do you notice how focused your mind is when you ask it empowering questions and make inspiring statements about this important area of your life. For example:

"How can I get more clients?"

"I'm excited to find more clients I love working with!"

You're probably also **visualizing** yourself attracting clients. You can see this on the internal movie screen of your mind. You're **investing** in mentoring, products, and books that are helping you to find better strategies, and you're **researching** online articles, **listening** to podcasts, and **watching** YouTube videos about the different subjects that will grow your business. See all the bolded verbs above? You are taking action! The wheels are turning mentally as you are processing all of the information that is available to you so you can better reach your goal.

Now we're going to expand the exercises to all the areas of your life so we can really start breaking down your formula We're going to look for recurring patterns of action and themes that demonstrate where your values lie. I want you to answer the following questions honestly. And don't overthink them!

Grab a piece of paper and write down the top three answers that pop into your mind for each question below, and list them in order of importance. When answering these questions, try to consider all angles. Think about what you spend the most time contemplating or visualizing or talking about. How do you spend your time, energy, and money? What are your dominant thoughts? What are your dominant feelings? What things or people in your life do you take inspiration from? Are there certain people you'd like to emulate?

Remember, for this exercise you need to write down your top three answers to each question below. Here are the questions:

### 1. Where am I spending most of my money?

Look at your bank statement and examine where most of your money going to. Look at these categories to get some ideas:

- Bills
- Business
- Body/Health
- Clothes
- Children
- Fitness
- Entertainment
- Travel
- Education
- Career

Once you have your top three answers, think about which of the seven areas of life each answer relates to. Write the name of each life-category next to your answer. For example, perhaps your top three answers are each linked to a different area of life, say, vocation/career/business, finance, and family. Or maybe all three answers lie within one realm, perhaps vocation/career/business.

**2. What am I saying to myself that is aligned with my goals and vision that is *demonstrating* my current reality?**

Let's say you want to make more money and you find yourself both taking action and telling yourself that this is what you want to do. This means you are in congruence, and therefore, you know it's important to you. Which areas of life do your top three answers specifically relate to?

**3. What am I reading online the most?**

What areas of life do your top three answers specifically relate to?

**4. What subjects am I reading about the most when I read books?**

Which areas of life do your top three answers specifically relate to?

**5. What podcasts, shows, or other things am I listening to or tuning into the most?**

Which areas of life do your top three answers specifically relate to?

**6. What videos am I watching online the most?**

Which areas of life do your top three answers specifically relate to?

**7. What am I talking to my friends and family about the most? What do I always steer the conversation back to?**

Which areas of life do your top three answers specifically relate to?

**8. What role do I identify myself with the most? I am a mother, entrepreneur, philanthropist, fitness fanatic, political junkie, philosopher, feminist?**

Which areas of life do your top three answers specifically relate to?

**9. What am I affirming to myself that is aligned with who I am? Do my affirmations truly support my life unfolding the way I want it to?**

What are the top three words and phrases I say to myself? Which areas of life do they specifically relate to?

**10. What inspires me so much that I would automatically do it without external motivation and without using the words "I have to," "I should," or 'I must"? What do I always find the energy to do?**

Which areas of life do your top three answers specifically relate to?

**11. What places do I visit the most on a daily, weekly, or monthly basis?**

For example, are you going to the coffee shop every day and does that represent work/business or social time for you? Which areas of life do your top three answers specifically relate to?

**12. Where am I spending most of my time on a daily basis?**

Which areas of life do your top three answers specifically relate to?

**13. What things are with me at all times?**

Which areas of life do your top three answers specifically relate to?

**14. What is in my living space that I have the *most* of?**

Look around your home: what do you see? If you have a lot of books, what areas of life do they represent? Does your computer represent more of a social outlet or a vehicle for business/career pursuits? Do you have a lot of pictures on the walls, and if so do they represent your family? Or do you perhaps have a collection of art; if so, what feelings does the art generate in you?

Which areas of life do your top three answers specifically relate to?

**15. What people do I spend most of my time with?**

Which areas of life do your top three answers specifically relate to?

**16. Where am I organized and neat?**

Which areas of life do your top three answers specifically relate to?

Some of these questions may seem repetitive, but they all tie into decoding the recurring patterns and themes that represents your personal values. So let's see what this exercise has shown us.

Next, we're going to figure out the top three areas of your life. Review your sheet of paper and tally up how many times each of the seven areas of life was indicated. Your top three areas of life are the three categories that garnered the most tally marks. For example, lets say that after answering the questions above, a great many of your answers clustered around spending money on business, reading business books, purchasing business coaching, thinking about your business frequently, spending a lot of time at your office, etc. This would indicate that the Vocation/Career/Business category is one of the top three areas of highest value to you. Once you have your top three areas figured out, see if you can rank them from 1 to 3. If you happen to have a tie between two or more areas, just ask yourself this question: what does this area of life really *represent* to me in terms of passion and commitment? Just drill down and keep it simple and you'll figure out the ranking.

You might wonder how you can be sure that the assessment is correct. If you answered the questions thoughtfully and honestly, it almost certainly is. But if you're still in doubt, ask yourself clarifying questions, such as "Does my life currently demonstrate consistent action in the areas of my top three list?"

If you're currently taking action in the top three areas of life you came up with from this exercise, that's an indication that you've done the assessment correctly and that your life is already unfolding—at least to some degree—according to your values. You know deep down inside what your life is revealing to you, but no one has really asked you these types of questions or tried to give you permission to be who you really are. Now you know.

If you still have doubts about the assessment, is it possible you did the exercise coming from a frame of mind of "I should/must" be doing this, and writing down answers accordingly? If so, you should redo the exercise. I will tell you a secret: anytime you use imperative language like "I should" or "I must," it is not reflective of your personal values. The reason people do this is because they take on values from other people and from society and try to pretzel those values into their own lives—when in fact these values just aren't *them*. I know, because I did the same thing for most of my life until I discovered the unique formula to unleash my "fabulous." All along, all I had to do to achieve my goals was to live by my own, true rules. How cool is that? So don't be hard on yourself, just start being the true you. You need to give yourself a break and give yourself permission to be yourself. It's freeing, it's tremendously empowering, and it's what you're here to do. Don't let anyone take that from you.

I know, easier said than done, right? Yes, however I will guarantee if you follow your personal formula you will be who you are and blaze your own trail of uniqueness and people will take notice. Whether you have a business, you're a full time mother, or you're a professional, your power will come from you "owning" it, from fully embracing yourself and what you believe. If you have kids, they will observe the way you conduct yourself and learn the valuable lesson that you are a woman who loves herself and knows what she's worth; that you're following your deepest desires and passions in life. You need to lead by example, because if you don't you'll succumb to the influence of others, take on their values, and lose yourself. Don't be the woman who throws her goals and dreams down the drain because her family doesn't understand her. Don't be the woman who needs the approval of the entire world. All you need to know is that being true to yourself will make you free, aligned, and on fire.

*"We realize the importance of our voices only when we are silenced."*
*—Malala Yousafzai*

**Italian Family Values**

Italians highly value their families, as demonstrated through the art of family meals. Every Sunday when I was living in Italy, I saw families take the entire day off to prep food and sit down to early dinners that lasted for hours. The food was typically homemade and served in three or more courses. During my Sunday walks, I would have a glimpse of their lives by peering through the windows to see big families taking time out to dine and connect.

### The Secret to Improving Any Area of Your Life

Next, what I want you to do is, for each of the seven areas of life, give yourself a rating from 1–7, 7 representing the highest state of fulfillment and competence. For example, if you were to rate yourself a 1 on finances, that would tell me you're not focusing on that area and it's where you have the hardest time. It may be uncomfortable for you to give yourself low scores, but don't worry; later I will share with you how to raise that score by creating goals that will inspire positive action. But for now just give yourself an honest assessment about what your life is actually demonstrating in each area. Keep in mind what I said before about how it's your actions—not your words—that give you a true reading on how congruent your life is with your values. Creating an honest snapshot of your life will help you change any area that you feel needs improvement. These types of mental exercises take work, I know, but it's all going to be worth it once you understand your unique La Dolce Vita Formula. You have to know where you're at before you can reprogram your mind for success.

**Rate yourself on a scale from 1-7 (7 means you are 100 percent fulfilled in that area of life)**

1. Life Purpose ____
2. Family/Relationship ____
3. Friends ____
4. Finances ____
5. Fitness ____
6. Mindset ____

7. Vocation/Career/Business ___

If you've found after you've done this exercise that you've scored pretty low in all areas, don't feel bad. It's just where you're at right now. The future will be different. When I was a fitness professional, I would assess a woman's body fat, weight, and current nutrition program. Oftentimes my clients didn't like having this done because of the somewhat depressing information this assessment revealed, but I changed the way they saw their numbers once I gave them the formula to reshape their body and mind. It was amazing to see the results they earned in just sevens days by changing simple things in their diet and exercise program. As we kept measuring, their numbers improved, and that fueled their desire to keep on track. I'm sharing this with you so you can realize that no matter what has happened to you in the past, and no matter what your current "numbers" are, you can improve in any area of life once you understand your unique formula.

One of the reasons why I get women such amazing results with their bodies is because I had been overweight myself. It's something I struggled with for many years. In fact, there was a time when I wanted to take my own life because I saw how much weight I had gained. I was thoroughly miserable. I had a high personal value of trying to figure out my own body's formula, but I had been getting nowhere. The old-school nutrition of the food pyramid didn't fit my body type. So I researched and studied for hours. I guess you could say I became my own science experiment, as I kept trying to find a formula for fat loss that would work.

In the end, I was able not only to find that formula, but I went far beyond and took my body to another level of lean. My values were so strong in the area of fitness and health that I started competing in bodybuilding and fitness contests. I won the title for Ms. Midwest States Natural and went on to frequently place in the top five in various bodybuilding, fitness, and figure competitions. It was one of the most challenging things I had accomplished up to that point in my life, but it was among the most rewarding, too. I have a clear memory of standing on the stage during my first bodybuilding competition. I wasn't the leanest and I didn't have the most muscle, but I looked amazing for me. I received the third place award that night, and I cried on stage while holding my 3-foot trophy, my mind flashing back to all of those dark years when I hated my body. That night I said to myself, "If I can do this, I can do anything!" I wanted to freeze-frame that moment in time because it set the stage for the other goals and dreams that I later pursued.

One of those resulting goals, mentioned above, was to help other women with their bodies. I took the science I developed to heal my own body and turned it into a system called the 6 Week Fat Burning Mind and Body System for Women over 40. I sold it online and held classes in my office. It was a hit, and I even wrote a bestselling book about the system that I still sell today called *Body of Love*.

So I know how you feel if you're not loving some part of your life right now, and I promise you that you have the power to change. So hang in there with me as I throw out your old rules for being stuck and stagnant and help you devise a new way of living that is inspiring to you. All you have to do is make a decision about what area(s) you want to work on and watch what happens.

My mission is helping women to become empowered in all seven areas of life. Having been disempowered myself, I know how it feels when you don't hit your goals, and what it's like to feel unfocused and overwhelmed, to be constantly putting yourself down. That's why I've dedicated my life to human behavior research and to designing the right technology and tools for women just like you, so you can achieve what you truly desire in life. Right now you are at the starting point.

Your highest values are not only the key to knowing what's important to you, they will help you to achieve the goals that you most highly desire. To clarify, the seven areas of your life correspond to your values. You will have a higher rating in the areas that you are taking action on the most and that you are thinking about, dreaming about, and making plans about. You know what your top three highest personal values are, and you've rated yourself in the seven areas of your life. I want you to start thinking about what you want to do, to be, and to have in your life that would make you feel fulfilled in every way. Don't hold back, either, because you deserve to live your La Dolce Vita life. So let's find your formula!

*"To be extraordinary, stop acting ordinary."*

## The Secret to Living a Fulfilling Life

Can you now see how knowing your values is the key to living a fearless and fulfilling life? I've worked with women (and men, too) all over the world, showing them how to design an inspiring life by uncovering their unique formula for life. Most people don't really know who they are, and as a result they beat themselves up constantly over their unmet goals. When you set goals that are aligned with your personal values, you'll find yourself taking consistent action. You'll wake up feeling inspired to do what you need to do to pursue your goals. The mental component of the La Dolce Vita Formula, which I will talk about later in this book, plays an important part in keeping you on track. In fact, the single biggest thing you need to understand is that your mind can empower you or sabotage you. This understanding is crucial if you want to achieve your goals.

If you fail to discover and follow your unique formula, you'll find yourself being misaligned in one or more areas of your life. When you set unrealistic expectations for yourself, you won't hit your goals and you'll stay stuck. You'll always be down on yourself and will eventually settle for an unsatisfying life. Let me illustrate this with a story about one of my clients. This client came to me wanting to build a $500,000 business in one year. The problem with this expectation was that she had yet to make her first $100,000. Also, one of her highest values was to be married and start a family. After I put her through exercises similar to the ones you did earlier in this chapter, it became clear that she wasn't taking massive action in the direction of her business. I helped this client understand her business goal was an unrealistic expectation because it wasn't actually among her top personal values. It's worth repeating: it's not what you say, it's what you do that indicates your personal values and creates your destiny.

By the way, did you know that staying true to your own path is also important to your physical health? Have you ever known someone who constantly gets sick, suffering one ailment after another? Their immune system is so weak that it seems just as they get over one thing they're afflicted with something else. You create disease in your body when you're not being true to who you are. Your body is trying to send you a message, to get your attention. How do I know this? I've interviewed and studied with some of the world's leading experts in epigenetics (the study of how our mental and physical environments affect our gene expression), and learned that we can actually turn on the switch in our genes for creating sickness and disease through our highly charged negative perceptions and mental states.

I interviewed Dr. Bruce Lipton, author of *The Biology of Belief*, who shared with me his discoveries about the interactions between the mind and body and the processes by which cells receive information. He explained how genes and DNA do not control our biology, that instead DNA is controlled by signals from outside the cell, including the energetic (and often very negative!) messages emanating from our thoughts. This is why it's important to realize how powerful your mental state is, in both creating the good things in your life, as well as harming your body with self-defeating thought patterns.

The highest value of one of my clients, "Amy," was to be in a fulfilling relationship. She was in her fifties, and the man she was married to was much younger and his values were radically different. There was constant tension in the relationship because she wanted him to be there more, and because his highest values were related to pursuing his vocation as a doctor. He spent long hours working at this instead of being present with Amy. I had Amy examine her values, which we contrasted to what his appeared to be. He would tell her one thing, but his values dictated another. In other words, his actions did not match his words. I help many women in their relationships with this one particular thing. They fixate on what a man is saying instead of what he is doing, then pay the price. Amy got so frustrated trying to change him and pretzeling herself for him that she started to resent him. The pain of not living a fulfilling life and being in a draining relationship was torturing her on an emotional level, to the point that she couldn't sleep, focus, or function. Her hormones were out of equilibrium because she was not feeling balanced internally That's why it's important to see your body as a feedback mechanism to your conscious mind. Take heed when you body is trying to get your attention!

I did a personal values assessment for Amy and her husband, after which she was finally ready to see the truth. She was tired of settling and not having her own values met, so she faced a very challenging situation: she had to get a divorce. This can be a tricky situation to navigate around emotionally, but once she identified what her true values were and then gave herself permission to live life in accordance with them, things changed immediately. First and foremost, all of the stress that was balling up inside of her went away. This was a great step forward for Amy at a time when so many areas of her life had seemed to collapse.

I was able to help Amy shift how saw herself, which allowed her to realize she was worthy of finding someone who was a better match. I told her as soon as she valued herself and made a *decision*, the men would start lining up. And guess what? They did. I laughed when she messaged me to let me know she had a date with someone who was actually older than her, someone whose values were more in alignment with how she wanted to live her life. She finally figured out her formula and will never go back to second-guessing what she can or can't have.

Take a moment to inventory all the things weighing on your shoulders, the things that you need to address but still haven't made a decision about. What's holding you back? Can you see when you don't advocate for yourself that you will feel stuck emotionally and physically?

I find that women suffer the most when they don't make decisions based on what their true values are showing them. If you pay close attention to your mind and body, you will always be guided in the right direction. Later in this book I will show you how to tap into your power and intuition. Realize that you have the power to change your life and your emotions, and to go after and get what you truly want. Don't let anyone tell you that you have to settle. More importantly, don't settle yourself.

Stay on your path and realize it's okay to feel off-balance at times, because that's the signal to re-sync your life. Matter of fact, I don't believe that you'll always be and feel balanced. There will always be something calling you, something based on your desires that is trying to get your attention. Don't buy into the belief that balance is the key, because sometimes being unbalanced will actually help you go to the next level in your life. Stop beating yourself up for feeling emotional. The key is not to remain in a negative mental state that you can't shift away from. Use your emotions as guidance toward where you want to go in life, and also as raw fuel to propel you in that direction, to get yourself to take action.

I also advise that you redo the personal values assessment you did earlier from time to time to keep it current. Certainly you should reassess yourself before taking on any new goal. And if you keep running against the wall when setting goals, use the personal values assessment to clarify if those goals are aligned with who you really are. If you find yourself using words like "I have to" or "I must," know that those words are not coming from true inspiration—because when you are inspired, no one and no thing is required to persuade you to go after what you really want.

**Fearless and Fabulous Female Profiles**

**Samantha Cristoforetti** (born 1977) is the third woman ever, and the first Italian, to join the European Space Agency. In 2014, she reached the International Space Station, and went on to establish the European and female records for length of stay in space (199 days). She received the title of "Cavaliere di gran croce dell'Ordine al merito della Repubblica Italiana," the highest Italian honor.

"Sometimes an obstacle is only a message of life. You have to find it another way, it doesn't mean you can't reach your target."
—Samantha Cristoforetti

Samantha is a great example of a fearless female who wasn't going to let anything stop her from pursuing her goals. She followed her formula and became an inspiration to all women who, figuratively or literally, are reaching for the stars. Try seeing yourself expanding in who you are and what you can be. Envision yourself as equal to extraordinary women like Samantha.

## Chapter Summary

The first step to uncovering your La Dolce Vita Formula is to discover your highest values in life. Recognizing your most important values will steer you unerringly toward goals and objectives that will naturally align with who you are as a person. In contrast, focusing on goals that lie outside of your values leads to friction, frustration, and, usually, failure.

In this chapter, you went through exercises to determine the three areas in your life that you consistently take the most action in. Your highest values are congruent with those areas. You then rated your level of fulfillment in each of the seven areas of life, which gave you a basic understanding of where you currently are in terms of inspiration and competence. This information will help you know where to concentrate your efforts in the future as your learn and follow your unique La Dolce Vita Formula.

# Chapter Two
# Desires: Creating What You Want

*"Be Fearless in the Pursuit of What Sets Your Soul on Fire" — Unknown*

## Understanding Your Power and Unlocking Your Potential

In the last chapter, I shared with you your unique formula for identifying your personal values. Think of your values as being the life force that fuels your soul. When you live by it, you are able to set, create, and achieve your deepest, most meaningful goals because you're living your life by what inspires you the most. Whenever you feel your life is headed in the wrong direction, your personal values will be there to guide you back, to help you rethink what is most important to you and realign yourself accordingly. After I realized this formula for myself and understood the magnitude of its force, I knew I had to communicate it with others, whether they were clients, my relationships, my family, and anyone that I met.

Understanding the power of values helped me to appreciate others for who they were. I stopped trying to make people "wrong" if their values were not aligned with mine, and I became more curious as to how their own personal formulas had evolved. On the other hand, I take a stand for myself if people are imposing their values onto me, and so should you. If you're asking a vegetarian to eat meat, realize that no matter how many reasons you come up as to why they should eat meat, you won't win them over. It's disrespectful of what is most meaningful to them. Give yourself a permission pass to be the most authentic version of yourself, and extend the same courtesy to others.

Imagine living in a state of never trying to pretzel yourself for anyone, even your family and friends. You can let go of stress and the never-ending quest for approval once you finally know who you are and are no longer willing to compromise yourself. You've gained the wisdom of knowing that if you go against your formula, then your body will get your attention in the form of stress, sickness, or disease. Your finances will go sideways, your mind will feel out of order, and every other area of life will be disrupted. Bottom line: you must train people how to treat you. It's all about understanding your own power.

If you find that your family or friends demand more of your time than you're willing to give, then you have the power to give yourself permission to say no, and be okay with an unfavorable reaction. If you have kids, owning your power will teach them the value of having personal time and boundaries, and of respecting that of others. After all, you're not responsible for their emotions. You are responsible to own your power, and realize that you have a choice about how to spend every single moment of every day.

*"Realize that you have a choice about how to spend every single moment of every day."*

Failing to own your power is like trying to drive a car that has very little gas in it. You won't get very far and when you finally run out you'll stop, stall, and feel frustrated. You'll start resenting others, but most of all you'll feel disappointed in yourself. When I am working with private clients, I like to speak in the language of their personal values, and I am careful to not inject my own beliefs based on my own personal values. My clients might not want to make a million dollars, be a size 4, or travel the world. Regardless of what they are after, they feel respected by me because when you learn about someone's personal values, you stop being judgmental and making people wrong for being who they are. We must all stop putting labels on people and love them for who they are. Help others to find their own formulas for fabulous living. This is a basic human need that is so often overlooked.

All too often, I come across coaches or consultants in this field trying to motivate their clients by inserting their *own* personal values into their teaching. It's a recipe for disaster, because people are yearning to express their own authentic selves. I've worked with clients from a wide variety of cultures, ethnic backgrounds, and belief systems, and I have tried to give each one my utmost respect. My job is to get them aligned to their own unique formulas by asking them specific questions that will inspire them and give them permission to live fearlessly and fabulously. I will ask them simple questions like, "What do you really want? What do you really desire but maybe you're afraid to go after and create? Why do you specifically want that?"

This leads me to asking *you* the same questions: What do you want to create that you feel you've lost sight of or can't seem to achieve? What do you feel confused about when trying to achieve your goals and dreams? Do you feel capable of so much more, yet find there's something stopping you from going to the next level of fulfillment in your life? If so, you'll find Chapter 4: Changing Your

Mental State to be very helpful. It will give you insights into your unconscious mind and reveal what's really been standing in your way. Trust me: finding out those mental blocks is half the battle.

I'm so excited to be sharing this information with you because for most of my life I, too, have been blocked and confused. Plenty of times I've beat myself up for not living to my highest potential. I hid in my fear, played small, and didn't take action. My feelings of living in a meaningless void drove me to seek out exactly what you're looking for, too. I want to help you uncover and create the right formula for you. There's no one else out there like you, so appreciate all that you have, every moment, and have faith that there is a unique formula for making your life work.

*"In order to be irreplaceable, one must be different." —Coco Chanel*

**Masters of Persuasion**

From food vendors, to clothing store associates, to cobblers, to restaurant managers, Italians are masters of the art of persuasion. They can convince you that everything tastes and looks *Che bello!* Their enthusiasm was convincing enough for me not only to take notice when I was there, but to buy (and buy and buy).

The Italian flair for persuasion taught me valuable lessons about how to share my passion about my products and services. When you communicate with enthusiasm and conviction, even the lowliest street vendor can sell like crazy.

## The Peril of Giving Away Your Power

Do you believe you have the power to create the life you want? If not, what evidence are you seeing to support that negative belief? If you're feeling disempowered, realize that mental framework is just a story you are telling yourself; it's a belief you are buying into. There are three things in life you have the power to control: your decisions, your perceptions, and your actions. It might seem hard to believe, but I bet if I could see the complete timeline of your life, I could show you the situations where you lost your power because you simply didn't believe you had it. These would have been times when you caved and probably beat yourself up. I can understand this more than you know because I played that role many times in my life. Once I found a way to own my power, it became much easier for me to not permit events or people to overpower me. You, too, have the power to create the life that you want. You can learn how to work with your energy in a way that is fun and exciting.

When you give away your power you're no longer in control of your life, and it becomes hard to make impactful decisions because you lack control. As a result, you start living in chaos and attracting more obstacles, things which get in the way of you aligning yourself with the true you (I will discuss how you attract chaos later in this book). So to reiterate, whenever you allow yourself to be knocked off course, off your unique formula, you won't be able to set goals and live authentically and congruently with your values. You'll be adrift in life and at the mercy of others.

According to an article in *Scientific American*, one in six people take a psychiatric drug, antidepressants being the most common. I've worked with clients who have come to me on medications such as these, but who then made the decision to stop using them because I helped them to realize that they have the power to change their own mental state and perception. Because your perceptions store memories and create illusions, they can sometimes have a negative impact on your physiology. William James, a famous American philosopher and psychologist who was also trained as a physician, said, "The greatest discovery of my generation is that a human being can alter his life by altering his attitudes."

The point I want to make is that every second of the day you're choosing how you want to think and feel. These are all factors in creating what you want in your life. Let's say your goal is to get in better shape, and you step on the scale one morning and see a number that you don't like. Before you set foot on that scale you were feeling great, but now your entire mood has suddenly shifted. Your day is shot and you start blaming yourself for your failures. But what if you had the awareness to understand that right in that moment you are giving your power away to an inanimate object—your scale? It would seem kind of silly, right? But as women we've been conditioned to think that our weight is our worth. It's complete crap and, honestly, weighing yourself is the most ridiculous way to measure your health and fitness. I feel this kind of thinking is an outdated practice that doctors and the healthcare system should get rid of entirely. I've always been on the cutting edge of fitness and fat loss, and I firmly believe it's time to stop living in the dinosaur world of having a number on a machine so greatly impact our lives.

When I was a fitness professional, I told women to go more by how they felt and how their clothes fit, and not to focus strictly on body fat. You can be a size 8 and weigh 160 pounds and look fit and fabulous in your clothes. My personal take on this subject is that if you are in alignment with your life, your emotions will be balanced. If your emotions are balanced, then you are more attuned to all the areas of your life. Conducting my own research and studying with some of the best in the field of self-perception has made me fiercely determined to help women worldwide discover the La Dolce Vita Formula and learn how to use it. Having a rewarding life means that you are following your deepest desires.

When I start working with a client and learning about her deepest desires, I ask her, "What would make your life amazing?" Many times they have no idea what they want, which is why I first have them perform a personal values assessment to establish a foundation for moving forward. Once I know who they really are, I am able to help them get clear on what they want, and, as a result, how to help them make empowering decisions that will move them toward their objectives. The art of making a decision is the springboard for birthing your desires, which in turn leads you to achieving your goals. When you follow the La Dolce Vita Formula, you start living your life in alignment. Watch out, world! I know that sounds easier said than done, but trust me, there is indeed a life-equation for getting what you want. You just have to understand and follow it. Of course, it's one thing to read about something and another thing to take action, so I will teach you how to get your mind and body in sync later in this book.

For right now, I want you to understand that your power lies in being able to make a decision. Let's say you want to leave a relationship that's not working. You know it's not working because you two keep fighting, and you feel sick, unfocused, and overwhelmed. The writing is on the wall, as everyone around you is trying to tell you, but you're not listening, not ready to take action. You keep making excuses and saying, "He might change, he might get some help." But you know deep down that your desires for what you want in a relationship aren't going to be met in this one. This relationship isn't going to work out. You feel like a failure because you think forcing yourself to stay is the better choice, and you've been comfortable being uncomfortable for so long that you hardly even know who you are anymore. You sense your thoughts and feelings are trying to guide you, yet you're living in the purgatory of not knowing and not making a decision.

As I've related, I can speak about this on so many levels because that was my story for many years. I didn't know how to make a decision based on my true desires, and I didn't realize that I could advocate for myself. As a result, I stayed in many unfulfilling relationships. Those relationships felt out of my control, and so did every other area of my life. Because I wasn't making a decision to leave those relationships, my business would go down and my bank account was barely breathing—all because I wasn't valuing myself. I had stopped paying attention to my desires. I felt mentally blocked, and the mental real estate of my mind was constantly occupied with "Should I stay?" or "Should I go?" thinking.

Years ago I was in one particular relationship where my indecision got the best of me. I was overwhelmed and miserable, and my body felt as if someone had poured cement on my legs. It was hard to get anything done on a daily basis. I cried every night when I went to sleep. I didn't do anything about the situation until I was jolted into a decision. That jolt was my aunt dying from stage four breast cancer. Her life was just about over, and I felt I was dying with her because of the choices I was making or failing to make. A day or two later my mom called me to tell me that Aunt Cheryl was in hospice and unconscious. Her boyfriend was in the room with her and had an engagement ring. He tried to slip it on her finger, but it wouldn't fit because her finger was enlarged by the fluid they were pumping through her body that kept her barely breathing. She was a body that was just existing in time and space.

I hung up the phone in tears. I knew her life would be over in a blink of an eye. My tears were as much for my own fears of dying because I was deciding to stay in a miserable relationship. A few days later my aunt passed away. I felt a surge of desire inside of me break out of this terrible rut and to own my power. I exclaimed aloud, "I don't want to get to the end of my life and not experience the love of my life!" It was one of the most powerful moments of self-understanding I've ever had, as I came to grips with what I was truly capable of, and realized with clarity that I had to make a decision for myself to get what I really wanted.

A few days later I rehearsed exactly what I wanted to say to my boyfriend: "I can't do this, I deserve more, I deserve to be loved for who I am. I know a man will love me for me. I no longer want to be in a relationship with you, and I'm choosing me!" That day a weight lifted from my feet and the sun shined through my soul, knowing my Aunt Cheryl was smiling at me because of my decision. I was back in alignment and started to visualize a new reality and new life. I started to formulate in my mind my La Dolce Vita life. Leaving that relationship and moving out on my own was the most liberating experience. My business got back on track. I made $100,000 in sales within 60 days, whereas before it took me anywhere from six months to a year to create that amount of income. I started dating and having fun and I met the man who I am going to marry. It was all because I broke through my fears, owned my power, and went after my desires.

If you're going through something like this experience right now, the first thing you *must* do is stop beating yourself up. Sometimes you have be in despair before you can look honestly at your desires. Learning this powerful lesson has helped me with my female clients. I can walk them through the steps from despair to desire to arrival at their destination. They feel powerful because I am not telling them they have to make an immediate decision; rather, I am asking them to see how they feel as a result of their current situation. I have them look at where they are giving their power away. I have them create a conscious connection so that they develop awareness. Creating awareness is the first step to being able to make a decision. And when you make a decision, you take a big step closer to your desires.

This formula works because it's not asking you to make an immediate decision, but rather to observe yourself—to gain information about how you think and behave. I've worked with women all over the world and I realize that women need to "feel into" a situation before they can make a decision about staying in or leaving a relationship. They like to talk, although if I find they go too much into a story I make sure I let them know. Why? Because repeatedly revisiting your story of what you don't want will not move you toward creating your desires. Stories can help get pent up emotions out of your system, but then we need to come up with an actual strategy. Personally, if I have a difficult issue in any area of my life I like calling one of my friends. I need to release what I am feeling; I'm not necessarily looking for a solution. I know the solution-seeking will come after.

It's been scientifically proven that women release the hormone oxytocin when talking or communicating. We love to talk about our problems, and when we do that we bond. However, don't get yourself into a pity party! Release . . . and then reset. The release you get from venting for a bit gives your body permission to remove stored-up negative energy. Once that release happens, you'll feel lighter and more grounded in both mind and body. Plus, you might get some good feedback, even if you're not looking for it, from the person your bonding with.

### How to Own Your Power

Let's take a look at your relationship to your power, with an aim to identifying where you are failing to own your power and what to do about it. When I am working with clients, one of the ways I get them results is to ask questions. You may have heard the quote, "The quality of your life is dependent on the quality of the questions you ask." This is exactly what you need to do in order to bring awareness to your conscious mind and address any imbalances you might have.

**How have you lost your power in the past? What about in the present?**

Look where you are currently giving away your power, or have done so in the past. Power can be lost to both people (spouses, children, business associates, etc.) and things (for example, a job that compels you to do things that don't fully resonate with your values).

What you want to do is take a hard look at where you have the most chaos and confusion in your life. What things are just not working? Perhaps it's an unfulfilling personal relationship. Or maybe some aspect of your professional life is dysfunctional. If you're an entrepreneur, are you giving your power away to crappy, entitled clients? Are you not charging what you're worth? Are you allowing people to walk all over you in your career and personal relationships? Look closely at your life and you discover where you're failing to own your power.

Take some time doing some hard thinking about these questions—an hour, a day, whatever you need. When you come back to this book, analyze what areas of your life are most impacted by your giving away your power. Similar to the exercise in Chapter One where you ranked the seven areas of life from 1–7 in terms of fulfillment and competency, this exercise will indicate which areas you need to grow stronger in.

**Start focusing on your power**

Now that you've identified areas of life where you are losing your power, let's flip the script and look at the positive. Think about times when you have acted in a powerful, purposeful way and achieved your goals. Are there areas in your current life where you are doing this? Here are a few questions to prime your mental pump:

- Where in your life have you stood up for yourself?

- What area of life was that in? What did you say or do in that moment?
- Is there an area in life right now where you are taking a stand and refusing to be compromised by the values of others?
- What exactly is it about your actions or behaviors that is making you powerful?

The point of this exercise is to make you aware that you can intentionally create patterns of action and thought to make yourself powerful. How? By understanding and mimicking what you did in the past when you successfully owned your power. There is a cause-and-effect mechanism for everything in our minds. Once you perceive what made you stronger in the past, you can duplicate that pattern in the present. Similarly, if you comprehend the areas of your life where you are weaker, you can disentangle the cause-and-effect mechanisms at play and learn not to repeat them. Looking for the *cause* is the key to reclaiming your power and getting back on track. Also, when you own your power there's a specific physiological–psychological feedback loop that takes place that syncs your body up with your goals. When mind and body are synced, you stay on target and create balance in your life (and regaining balance in the event you lose it becomes a much easier task, too).

### Understanding Your Desires

I asked you earlier to think about what you really want in life. If you still aren't crystal clear on this, don't worry, because right now I am going to help you explore your true desires. The process of doing this will go a long ways toward clarifying what you want. To begin, are there perhaps certain things you keep thinking you would like to accomplish? Maybe:

- Get in better shape and have more energy
- Attract better clients and make more money
- Find your life's purpose
- Change your profession
- Attract the right partner
- Increase your income
- Travel the world

Think back to a time in your life when you really wished something would happen, and *it did happen*. Do you recall what made you want the thing you wished for? Where were you? How old were you? What were you thinking about at the time? What were you feeling? How long did it take for it to happen?

**Fearless and Fabulous Female Profiles**

**Artemisia Gentileschi** (1593–circa 1656) was one of the first female painters in Italian history. Her main inspiration was the painter Caravaggio. She also learned from her father, Orazio, who was a painter, too, and from the Roman painter Agostino Tassi. Tragically, Tassi brutally raped Artemisia. After this painful episode, she decided to moved to Florence, where she studied the masterpieces of Michelangelo, and from there to Venice, Naples, and London. Artemisia showed how a woman could excel in the sexist society of the XVII century. The protagonists of her works were often women who overcame men, as depicted in her painting *Giuditta* and *Oloferne.*

Sometimes our desires can be formed out of what we perceive as bad situations. The secret is to never let events define you; rather, use them to empower you to learn and grow. Artemisia had a challenging life, but in the end she didn't let men overpower her. Don't let anyone conquer your mind and deter you from your destination. In my work, I have helped women transform their shame, guilt, and trauma surrounding challenging situations that were holding them back into positive "fuel" to help them get back on track and reach their highest potential.

Doesn't it feel empowering to think back to that very moment when you *decided* to take the steps you took? And perhaps there were challenges you overcame in the process. Now, fast-forward to the moment when you achieved your goal. Don't you relish reliving the experience? Doesn't it make you want to strive for more?

I've told you that one of my deep desires was to improve my fitness and health, to create my ideal body. As I mentioned, I decided I wanted to compete in a bodybuilding competition. What got me started on this path was attending an event where my boyfriend at the time was competing. When the women came out on stage, I had a strong sense of certainty and desire that this was something that I wanted to do. I didn't know how I was going to do it, but I just knew that I would. And I also knew that it would take hard work to get there, but I didn't care. My desire was so strong that I knew I would master the art of daily discipline and dedication.

As it turned out, the total prep time from start to finish took me about four months. The day of my first competition was exciting and nerve-wracking; as a beginner, I didn't know what to anticipate. But then I was standing on stage and in that moment felt I was in complete alignment. I had set a goal and actually achieved it. This sensation was something completely foreign to me, since I had never competed in a bodybuilding show, let alone followed a strict diet and exercise regimen. In fact, I had spent many prior years going on diets, only to gain the weight back. I would always find a way to sabotage my own efforts. It was an endless cycle of feeling defeated, and it seemed that no matter what, I couldn't figure out how to crack the formula to get my body in shape. Now, standing on the stage before the crowd, all those disappointments seemed like someone else's dismal past.

I want you to embody this same sort of energy. Take yourself back and recall some of your inspiring, powerful memories. Survey your childhood, high school, college, and beyond. In your mind, go to that time and place of success and relive how you felt in your body. Reconnect to the thought process you then had, as this helps you to bring forth proof to your current conscious mind that you *have* accomplished meaningful goals before, at times when you were acting in alignment with who you really are. Know that you are still the same person deep inside, and you can win again.

Realize that there is a powerful force inside of you that knows she can do it, and that this force is part-and-parcel of the formula for creating anything you want. Think of your desires as the fuel for being inspired. Imagine waking up each day and following your desires, taking action, and achieving your goals. How would that make you feel?

This is a good point for me to better explain what I mean by *desire*. A desire is a strong feeling of wanting to *have* something, or *wishing* for something to happen. We all have plenty of wants and feelings like this, so I advise you to write down your deepest desires, the ones you keep dreaming about, even if they feel outrageous. The reason I want you to write these down is that all too often we let other people dictate what we *should* or *shouldn't do*, and *can* or *can't* have. You need to clearly know your own desires to avoid that trap. However, you can't act on all of your desires; some are much more worthy of pursuit than others. In the next section I will show you which of your desires to go after—based on the personal values you uncovered in Chapter One—the ones that will help you to live your La Dolce Vita. When you pick the right desires to go after, you will actually achieve them, instead of creating unrealistic expectations that result in you berating yourself because your dreams haven't materialized.

### Choosing Your Desires

The exercises below will help you determine your deepest desires. Have fun with this! Be creative and playful. We're going to go back to our list of the seven areas of your life, but this time we'll view them in light of your wants and wishes. Write down one to three strong desires that you have for each area. As always, take your time. The higher the quality of thinking you do now, the better the ultimate result.

1. **Life Purpose**
   My desires:

2. **Family/Relationship**
   My desires:

3. **Friends**
   My desires:

4. **Finances**
   My desires:

5. **Fitness**
   My desires:

6. **Mindset**
   My desires:

7. **Vocation/Career/Business**
   My desires:

Now that you have brainstormed this list, scrutinize what you've written. Which desires speak to you the most? Which ones do you feel you would love to do or conquer? Which ones would make you feel the most fulfilled, if you were to achieve them?

**Fearless and Fabulous Female Profiles**

**Fabiola Gianotti** (born 1960) fell in love with physics when she read about Einstein's explanation of the photoelectric effect. She joined the European Organization for Nuclear Research (CERN) in 1987 and became the coordinator of the ATLAS experiment in 1999. The ATLAS experiment seeks to investigate and explain subatomic particles. In 2012, she announced the discovery of the Higgs boson. Fabiola was elected Director General of CERN in 2014, the first woman appointed to that role.

*"Knowledge, as Art, is owned by humankind." —Fabiola Gianotti.*

Fabiola is a perfect example of a woman who made history by going after her desires. She was inspired by Einstein's work and pursued exactly what she was aligned to do. Spend a moment to think about similar women you've encountered or read about who achieved their goals. Who do you most admire and strive to emulate? How has their work fueled your own desires?

### Getting Crystal Clear on Which Desires and Goals to Go After

Have you ever set a goal that you haven't met? I know I have. In the past I would set unrealistic money goals for my business that didn't match who I was at that time. Each time I set a goal that I thought was achievable and then failed, I started to think that there was something wrong with me. It wasn't until I started to focus on understanding my unique formula that I was able to set goals that were in alignment with my values, goals that then became achievable. Soon I was setting even bigger goals, all congruent with my La Dolce Vita Formula.

I get sick of hearing other people, particularly life coaches, brag about how much money they are making, and then try to make you feel bad about yourself because you are not at their income level. I consider it to be false teaching because they are projecting onto you their personal values, as if your values should naturally match theirs. I was reading a book the other day by a woman I will not name, but someone very successful whose passion and drive I admire. However, the entire book seemed to be about telling the reader to just get over herself and realize she is just living in fear. I didn't find this inspiring. As I was reading, I found it interesting to observe that the author never mentioned the success formula for how to get out of your own way. Rather, the book was page after page of her ranting and dropping F-bombs. I felt like she was on an ego trip, trying to motivate others by saying, "Hey, you have to be like me, and if you're not, you are lazy." With this type of leadership, it's no wonder why we beat ourselves up so much by thinking we are not good enough. What I teach is the exact opposite, because as I've been saying all along, you have to follow your own formula. You have to live a life that is authentic and meaningful to you. Screw everyone else who tells you it's their way or the highway!

I want you to feel liberated knowing that there's nothing wrong with you if you've experienced these types of tactics, or if you've tried to set goals and each time you've taken first steps only to seem to sabotage your efforts. There's a reason why you didn't get to where you wanted to go, and berating yourself, or having someone else castigate you for having "unrealistic expectations," is a recipe for throwing in the towel and quitting for good. This is why I want you to get crystal clear on what you really want, and not what society is dictating, or what some person on Facebook or Instagram is telling you real success is.

Your La Dolce Vita life—your sweet life—has nothing to do with what other people have or think you should be, and everything to do with what you truly desire. I know it can be a challenge to not get caught up in the glitz and glamour that is part of modern life, and later in this book I will talk about the hazard of comparing yourself to others (which diverts you away from living your own magnificent life). Whether it's a celebrity, friend, or trying to keep up with the Joneses, realize you're on your own journey. All you have to do is focus on what you want. Nothing more.

**Beware the Social Media Time Thieves!**

According to an article on *Time Health* online, Instagram is one of the worst social media platforms for mental health, especially for the younger generation. As much as I like social media, I limit my consumption and urge you to do the same. Social media not only steals away your time, it gets you caught up in what I call "unicorn thinking" of how your life *should* be. Truth be told, many people on social media are putting on a façade of living a perfect life. If you were to follow them around twenty-four hours a day, you'd discover they have plenty of their own inner dragons to slay.

As human beings we will always experience full quantum, which means being exposed to both the pain and pleasure of life. This is why developing a firm knowledge of who you are is the single most important thing you can do if you want to create the life you love and do it on your terms. We all go through moments when we think we want something glitzy that we see in the media or online, but those are precisely the times when it's most important to go back to your personal values assessment and remind yourself about your top three personal values, which are the true guides to your life. You live your life by your top three values, which are demonstrated by *what* you do and not by what you say you are going to do.

For example, lets say you want to start a business, but every time you tell yourself that you are ready to take action you find that you're spending all of your time with your kids. There's nothing wrong with this, or course, just realize that your life is always demonstrating what your highest personal values are (your family, in this case). You want to make sure that what you say you want is in alignment with your highest values, otherwise when you try to set goals you'll end up feeling defeated and depressed because you didn't achieve what you said you would. However, if you can picture in the example above how taking action and creating your business will actually help fulfill your values in regard to being with your family, then your brain can make the connection to take action. Your brain is like a GPS system that is setting it's destination by what is most inspiring to you. If you don't follow that GPS you run into roadblocks and take major detours along the way.

Here's another example: let's say you tell yourself you want to get in better shape, yet you find yourself socializing instead of spending time at the gym. Knowing how you're wired is critical for setting and achieving any goal, so if you do in fact love socializing with friends, then setting an ambitious fitness goal might prove unrealistic because of how it will impact your social life. An initial goal of spending at least one day a week in the gym to start might be the solution to get you to start taking consistent action. And consistency is the key for making a habit stick. This is why I don't like setting New Year's Resolutions. They just don't work, and most people give up on them in the first month.

### Determining Your Top Three Desires

In the first chapter, you identified your top three personal values, and earlier in this chapter you listed your top desires for each area of life. Now we're going to match those two lists up to give us some insight about which goals you should pursue. The first thing I want you to do is take a hard look at the list of desires you wrote down earlier and try to determine your top three, just as you did with your values. What are the desires that truly inspire you, that would be truly fulfilling were they to be achieved?

Desire 1: ______________________

Desire 1: ______________________

Desire 3: ______________________

### Matching Desires and Your Highest Values Leads to Your Goals

Now, that you've identified your top three desires, let's see if any or all of them match your top three values that you previously determined. If there is at least one match, then congratulations! You now have a very strong indication of where to set your goals. It doesn't matter if they are "small" goals (in fact, that might be for the best when you're just getting started), what matters is that they are the right goals for you.

If you do this exercise and cannot come up with any matches, then I recommend you spend some time reconsidering the lists of desires and values you have put together before trying this exercise again. Odds are, your next round of results will be better.

You have now identified one or more major, life-fulfilling goals to go after, goals that are aligned with your values and deepest desires. Give yourself permission to go after these goals with everything you've got! Set you mind to it! My father always told me, "Heather, you can do anything you set your mind to." I didn't really understand what he was saying, as I was a child, but somehow it still made sense, because when I did focus and set my mind to do something that was aligned with my highest personal values, I accomplished it every single time. Those were some of the most powerful words of wisdom my father taught me. I remember having a conversation with him late one night about mindset and money. He said once I made my first million, it would be easy to make the next million. My father's lessons about focus and mindset changed the way I saw and generated money.

*"Give yourself permission to live an extraordinary life. Step into your greatness. Stop playing small. Live your truth."*

When I work with clients for an entire year, we look at setting goals and creating a vision for the rest of their life, but I also show them how to take *daily* inspired action steps so they can progress toward their goals without being overwhelmed. I put them through the exact formula of discovery I am sharing with you, but the reason why I am not having you look at your entire life's goals right now is that I find people do better once they start with one to three initial, often smaller goals. This gives them a chance to better see how the La Dolce Vita Formula works. After completing your smaller goals, you can then without a doubt set bigger goals. Your mind will start expanding because you're building more confidence each time you set and achieve your goals, however minor they may sometimes be. It took me years of being fed up and frustrated until I realized this for myself. I know sometimes life can feel like it's a race, but in actuality the more you slow down your mind the faster you will get to where you want to go. It might seem counterintuitive, but it's true. If you're a more ambitious person like me, then take on more accountability and additional goals. But do so only if you have personal values that are in alignment to support these efforts. You set the pace; it's not a race.

### Your La Dolce Vita Vision

Now it's time to get crystal clear on your goals, so that we can give them the best chance to materialize. The next step is to create what I call your La Dolce Vita Vision. I want you to take the one to three things that you want to achieve and define them with even more clarity. The clearer you are, the easier it will be for you to take the right actions. If you leave the details out of your vision, you'll experience uncertainty and, as a result, feel confused or overwhelmed.

Let me tell you a little story to elaborate on this. When I was doing an interview on CBS in San Francisco, the host asked me, "How do we set really good goals?" I told her that it's like going to a restaurant and asking the waiter or waitress for food. There's a level of uncertainty as to what exactly they will bring back. But when you are clear and specific about what your desire, it's easier to get exactly what you want. I think of it like this: You place your order to the Universe, and then you must take action on what the Universe delivers, no matter what it is. But if you are specific in your request, you're more likely to receive what you really want to get. So, instead of asking for "food," you say, "I will have a chicken breast, with a side of roasted brussel sprouts. And for my salad, can you put the dressing on the side?" Does this help you see how getting crystal clear on your objectives helps you visualize, conceptualize, and achieve them?

By way of further example, let's say one of your goals is to lose fifteen pounds. Since you know I hate scale-weight-oriented goals, I would recommend you focus on getting clearer on how you want to look in your clothes after you lose weight. What clothing size and body fat percentage would create the image you are looking for? Can you visualize with clarity what accomplishing your goal would look like? Work on the visualization until you can, and then create a timeline to achieve your goal that makes sense based on your schedule. It might take you longer to lose those last few pounds of fat, but if you want them off permanently, your goal-achieving process must be doable based on your current lifestyle.

I'm introducing the La Dolce Vita Vision here, but Chapter 6: Aligning Your Actions with Your Desires will provide further instructions on creating a great vision document for yourself.

### Your Driving Force: Knowing Your Why

Another important factor in achieving your goals is to create a "neuro link" in your brain. A neuro link is simply a neural connection that tells your brain *why* your goal is important. Creating a neuro link changes your brain's neuroplasticity and creates new neuro path ways, all of which help to strengthen your commitment to achieve your goals by making your action-steps nearly automatic

When I am consulting with clients who have businesses, I help them create neuro links for their sales processes. I use the following phrase: "No why, no buy." This means, if you don't know the driving force of what your customer or prospective client wants, they probably won't buy from you. It come down to basic human behavior: you must be able to know what's important to your customer in order for them to say "Yes" to you. It's almost never an issue of money, because people have the money for what they value the most. The example I like to give takes us back to the stock market crash of 2008. I was in an Apple store, which as you know is a luxury brand. Despite the gloomy financial news, the store was packed and people were whipping out their credit cards to buy premium Apple products. This is proof that you always have the time, energy, and money for what you value the most. Those people's actions were proof of this.

This leads me to ask you an important question: What's *your* driving force? *Why* do you want the things you wrote down earlier? If you were my client, and we were working together to help you achieve clarity, I would start by asking you these questions. If you couldn't answer right away, that would tell me there's not a driving force behind what you said you wanted. So then I would look at your top three personal values. If your relationship with your husband is one of your top three personal values, I would delve into a deeper subset of questions about your relationship, as well as the two other top areas, until I finally arrived at the right questions to ask to create neuro links in your mind. For example, "How will losing fifteen pounds of fat and being a size 8 by June 13th change your relationship with your husband?"

Neuroplasticity in the brain can occur in milliseconds when you ask the right, penetrating questions, question that help you to see how accomplishing y or doing x will lead you to be more fulfilled in that area. Asking the right questions is among the most powerful things you can do to achieve a balanced, ideal mental space. However, most people ask themselves the wrong questions, questions that are self-destructive and disempowering. For example, "Why can't I lose weight?" Or, "How is this time going to be different, since I've failed so many times before?" Or, "Why can't I handle my finances? And how come I keep attracting crappy relationships?" Trust me—that was my voice many years ago until I found the formula that set my life on fire. What you want to do is take your goals/desires, and your top three highest values, and ask yourself good, empowering questions until you link and sync your brain up. You know you've made enough links when you're inspired to take action. If you're not ready to take action, then you need to go back and ask more questions until you do feel ready to act.

**Find the formula to link and sync your brain by asking yourself this question**

How is having ________________ going to empower or help me

in the area of ________________?

You might have to ask yourself this question 100 or more times, but it works. I know it sounds repetitive, but in order to reprogram your brain you must be relentlessly repetitive so that you can establish the conscious connection that clearly shows how having what you want is going to help you fulfill that highest value. Repetition is key when introducing new concepts and making sure neuro linking takes place. You will start believing things the more you say them, and most importantly when there is meaning behind them. This is why asking yourself the question above multiple times is key to your success. In fact, the very act of asking this question means you're taking action, and have begun to move toward achieving your goals. Moreover, this isn't some ridiculous affirmation that isn't aligned with who you are. Since you're asking a question based on your unique formula, it's going to be much easier for you to rewire your brain. I can't tell you how many times I've recited the useless types of affirmations taught by others, but nothing ever materialized until I started using the brain technology described in this chapter. We will talk much more about these topics in the later chapter titled "Changing Your Mental State," so stay tuned.

For now, keep asking great questions that will get to your driving force and add detail and clarity to your goals. What is your why? Why is it important for you to actualize your dreams? What would achieving this particular goal do for you in the various areas of your life? Go up and down the list of your personal values in life and keep answering until you have tears of inspiration and feel in complete alignment.

Here are some example questions as pertains to your body (just modify them as needed to apply to other areas of your life, such as money, kids, or relationships):

- How will creating my ideal body help me in the area of my career/business?
- How is creating my ideal body going to help me in my area of family/relationship?
- How is creating my ideal body going to help me in the area of my mindset?

Keep asking the question and don't stop! Exhaust your mind until you've felt that internal clicking sound, meaning you're locked in. Outside forces can never provide the degree of motivation which comes from within. Internal inspiration is a more powerful fuel than anything else. When you are inspired, you automatically do with relish what you need to do to achieve your goals.

You never know how long you have on this planet, so why not live each day as your last? We tend to take so much in our lives for granted, and we get sidetracked on the most insignificant things in our life. When you give yourself permission to live an extraordinary life, there's no stopping you. You become a force for good and you radiate out into the world the essence of who you are, which in turn attracts the people and resources around you who can support your dreams. You feel like you're in the flow of life, instead of forcing and wishing things to happen. But these good things result from you doing the hard mental work of asking yourself penetrating questions and upgrading your brain by creating neuro links that inspire your conscious mind to take action. Those neuro links are your friends, and they'll keep you in the flow, even when things seem to be going sideways.

*"When you give yourself permission to live an extraordinary life, there's no stopping you."*

I was working with a client who was going through a divorce, and she resented her ex-husband for his cushy lifestyle, buying a yacht and taking luxurious trips around the world. A single mom with two children, she was left to fend for herself. One of the things that we worked on was training her to transform her resentment into the empowering emotions of gratitude and love. This concept is so important that Chapter 8 of this book is devoted to it. I asked my client to think about how working on her business, making money, and getting organized in her finances was going to empower her, especially when it came to taking care of and loving her two children. I kept asking her those questions in different ways so she would start to link and sync those thoughts in her brain. A few short weeks later, she was on her path to being empowered. She took daily inspired action on everything she needed to get done to transform her business and her life. She even had her kids take on some of the responsibilities that she felt overwhelmed and stressed about.

Can you seen now how this process of questioning, clarifying, and developing strong neuro links can help you? Your driving force is there to help assist you in owning your power and accomplishing things that might feel hard at first. I know you can do it. I've coached people through just about every issue you can imagine, and helped women empower all seven areas of their lives. If you have kids, asking yourself questions is particularly helpful in getting you to see how you are impacting them through your actions and behaviors. Your children will take notice of your example and follow in your footsteps.

To master anything, you must learn it yourself to the point where you are able to teach it to others. The learning process may take hours, sometimes a lifetime, but it's worth it if it leads to you becoming the woman you want to be: fearless, fabulous, and feeling fulfilled in her life. No one said that the journey was easy, but that's how a driven woman thinks. She believes in herself and goes after what inspires her the most, even though it might be tough at times.

**Chapter Summary**

In the first chapter, you uncovered your three highest personal values. This chapter took you through the next step of discovering your La Dolce Vita Formula by giving you exercises designed to uncover your deepest desires. These deep desires, when matched with your highest personal values, point you unerringly toward the goals you can not only pursue in life but also actually achieve. When your desires are aligned with your values, nothing can stop you!

# Chapter Three
# Identifying Obstacles and Solutions

*"Nothing is impossible, the word itself says 'I'm possible'!" —Audrey Hepburn*

In the last chapter, you asked yourself several important questions to get clear on your desires: What do I really want? What is my life truly demonstrating? You also strove to discover what force is driving your desire to achieve the things you want, in alignment with your personal values.

These are crucial first steps along the path that leads you to your goals, but there is more to consider. You will also confront obstacles along the way, and you need the tools to bypass or overcome them. Hate obstacles and challenges? Well, get used to them, because if you're a driven woman like me you must become immune to them. You must develop a thick skin, and see obstacles as being merely part of the process of finding and getting your way. I love reading the works of Marcus Aurelius, who was Roman emperor from 161 to 180. Aurelius was also a noted stoic philosopher, and I came across this quote from him while studying and living in Florence, Italy, that spoke volumes to me: "The impediment to action advances action. What stands in the way becomes the way." The obstacle you are facing *is* the way and what impedes you empowers you.

I remember when I first learned how to sell in my business. The concept of selling was new to me and the idea of being rejected was daunting. I kept hearing other mentors and people who were masters of the sales process say, "You must let go of the need for approval. You must develop thick skin." It took a while for me to develop the thick skin they are talking about. Early on, when I received hateful emails or messages from people telling me they didn't like the photos of myself on my website, I almost broke down. I just couldn't believe that people would say these things about me, since all I was trying to do was get my message out there about helping women live better lives. But in time, the thick skin came, and now I laugh at those types of emails. Today I love selling because to me it's about transforming someone's life. So I want you to figure out where you are breaking down in your life, where you wish things were easier. You have to be all in to get to your destination, because there will always be challenges in any area of life you want to master.

*"The question isn't who is going to let me; it's who is going to stop me.*
*—Ayn Rand*

There's so much wisdom we can learn from leaders, philosophers, and trailblazers who have paved their own path to greatness. We don't need to figure out everything ourselves. We just need to listen to them. They endured great challenges, which is why they've left their mark in history. Their words of wisdom have stood the test of time, and, believe me, they apply to you. Life will present you with many forms of obstacles. It's my goal to teach you the formula to overcome them.

## Obstacles I've Faced on My Path

For many years I tried everything that I could think of to make money in my previous businesses. I invested so much money that I almost gave up. There were times when I just wanted to throw in the towel. I was completely disempowered in the areas of money and men. But then I was faced with a situation that left me no choice but to face my biggest fears in life. It was 2 a.m. and I had a fight with my boyfriend. I had moved across the country with no car, a few hundred dollars in my bank account, and my little Chihuahua, Angel. Crazy, right? He threw me out. I didn't even know a soul and I had nowhere to go. I took what I had and threw it in trash bags. I sat in the dark feeling fearful and crying with Angel on my lap. How could I let this happen to me? I was a college-educated woman and had nothing to show for it. I kept attracting the same kinds of relationships, and I couldn't seem to get my life together. I was feeling pretty sorry for myself.

But that night something powerful happened. I didn't know what it was, but I had an inner knowledge that things were about to change. I made it my intention in that moment that I wasn't going to stay in my miserable situation. I would find a way out. I didn't know how I'd do it, but I somehow knew deep down that the obstacles I was attracting were there for a reason. It was the most humbling experience of my life. I was tired of living in constant fear and made a decision then and there to change. Have you ever gotten to the edge and told yourself that something has to change because you're tired of settling?

The very next day I found a complete stranger to move in with on Craigslist. Then I locked myself in my bedroom and went to work. I was going to succeed this time, and I was going to stop making excuses because my life depended on it. I had so much drive and desire, nothing was going to stop me. But I knew I couldn't do it alone. I needed someone to help me. I had my why, like I mentioned before, so I set an intention to find someone who could help me get out of my money mess. A week later I found a mentor who changed my entire financial life. My investment in her was more money than I'd ever made in a year, but when your why is strong the how's take care of themselves. I managed to find some money on one of my credit cards. Yes, I know that funding your life through debt and credit is not the smartest decision. Or was it? I got results.

I won't claim that my the path is the right path for you to take; but it was the right decision for me at that desperate point in my life because what happened in the next six months was life-changing. The only thing I did during those six months was work, workout, sleep, and repeat. I committed myself to having success, because I was beyond ready to break the self-destructive patterns afflicting my life and find the formula to make money and have fulfillment. During this time I didn't date at all, because that would have been a distraction. What I did do was create a vision board with a car on (I didn't have one at the time and I was riding the bus). My vision board gave me more drive and fuel to get my act together.

After six months, it wasn't until I was doing my taxes that I realized I had made over $100,000 during that half-year period. This realization shattered my financial paradigm of what was possible for me, because previously I was only making around $16,000–$30,000 a year. Having a mentor who believed in me was a crucial part of my turnaround; she showed me how to take control of my mindset and take massive action with the right plan. I was so busy that there was no time to wallow in fear or ask myself, What if this doesn't work out? My mind was set on doing whatever it was going to take to reach my goals.

This was way before the internet was at the stage it was today, so I had to be innovative with my ideas. I created and sold programs before the programs were even completed. In other words, I was selling ideas first because I knew I could make them happen once I had the sales. There was value in what I was offering my clients, and I wasn't going to let anyone or anything get in my way—including myself. I wanted to make a difference and help others. To improve what I had to offer, I started studying quantum physics, brain science, and anything I could get my hands on to advance my level of knowledge. This effort helped my client, and it also helped me. I didn't even have a marketing budget, so I learned to be creative and scrappy to make things work and get the word out there. Soon, people all over the world began to reach out to me, and I helped them get unstuck. The results were liberating for both them and me. I felt I had a purpose on this planet.

Flashing forward, I was able to move into my own place, with my own car. I felt proud that I was able to turn my life around. Interestingly enough, one night I saw that old boyfriend who threw me out at a bar we used to frequent. He looked as white as a ghost when he noticed me, and I could tell by the look on his face that he'd been carrying around guilt and shame for what he had done. He told me, "I'm so sorry, Heather, for throwing you out. Please forgive me." I actually thanked him and said, "Please don't feel sorry. What you did actually changed my life. My business is successful and I love my life!" He had a look of disbelief on his face, but it didn't bother me. I was aligned with my dreams and empowered. His opinion of me no longer mattered. Can you believe he actually wanted to get back with me, too? Lesson learned. Next!

I often look back to that situation, that big set of obstacles that I overcame, and think about how those experiences became a major part of my personal life-formula. I was able to be true to myself and own my power. I realized that when I follow my own path and what's inspiring to me then my life flows. And when I go against myself and don't make choices that are aligned with my highest personal values, I attract chaos and confusion. I wouldn't be writing this book today and speaking to women worldwide about my story if I hadn't lived through that period. Yes, I've been disempowered from everything from money to men, but I've made it my mission in life to empower millions of women by sharing with them my story and, more importantly, the formula to create their La Dolce Vita Life. My story is unique, as is yours. Maybe you haven't encountered obstacles in the forms of men or money, but I can guess if you're reading this you're facing obstacles of one sort of another in different areas of your life. Perhaps your efforts to get in better shape keep attracting obstacles that get in your way (usually in the form of self-sabotage). Or perhaps your obstacles lie in the areas of spirituality or family. Regardless of what exactly you're confronted with, know that most of these obstacles are generated by you, and not external forces. If you can understand this, you can overcome the roadblocks in your way. This is what I want to explore with you next.

### How Your Unconscious Mind Attracts Obstacles

Earlier in this book, you learned about your personal values—your internal driving forces that you must follow—and created a list of your top three. Knowing your values is critical to the success of the La Dolce Vita Formula. If you don't know what your values are, you'll without a doubt attract obstacles.

Let's try a little exercise to demonstrate this. Think about an area in your life right now where you are unorganized, and this messiness is attracting chaos. Or think of a similar troubling situation from your past. I want you to concentrate and connect the dots of the Law of Cause and Effect. Since you were not empowered and ordered in this area, have you attracted someone into your life who has only worsened the situation? Or has the chaos in this area resulted in your failing to pay enough attention to some other important part of your life? Can you see how failing to deal with one part of life often attracts additional problems? Sometimes we don't recognize this Law of Cause and Effect, and we shove the root problem deep down in our unconscious so we can avoid taking action to change it. However, this doesn't alter the fact that your chaos will always be in your face, confronting your conscious mind.

I was living with a boyfriend who was extremely unorganized in his finances and would spend money on frivolous things. This was after I had straightened out my financial life, as detailed above, so we had major disagreements over money because I never wanted to go back to that painful place again. This is one value of mine that will never go away because I now understand and appreciate money, and I enjoy working hard on my business. The true degree of his financial situation wasn't clear until he kept getting bank fees for having zero dollars in his account. What I found to be interesting is that he attracted me into his life to get his sh#t together. Thanks, Universe! (With a bit of sarcasm.)

I have to laugh at this because that's how life works. I actually taught him to be more responsible with money, how to do sales, and how to market himself through speaking and networking. I challenged him to get off his butt, start paying attention, and get serious. He was so used to his cushy lifestyle that when he bought a business that already had clients attached to it, he soon sold it without considering the value those existing clients gave him in the brand new industry he was getting into. So he had to learn how to acquire clients from the ground up and run things like an actual business. This was hard work, because his values were more oriented toward socializing and acquiring objects. As you can guess, it was draining for me to be with him. But by attracting him I did learn an important lesson, which was to value myself as a woman and know that I was worthy of being with a man who was more aligned with me in all areas of life. I don't have any regrets about this boyfriend because I realize that if I took him out of my life's equation, I wouldn't have met my now soon-to-be-husband, Ed. Sometimes I look at life and have to laugh because I now understand how, as I've evolved as a person, I've attracted each of the players in the different stages of my game of life. I realize that I have the power to rewrite my present and future.

This is why no matter what's happened to you in the past, it's necessary for you to grow and change as a person. How you perceive each situation in your life is critical in creating the vision of what you want moving forward. Even bad things from your past can play a helpful role in this. I will be sharing with you how to change the way you look at your past later in this book, because it's your perceptions that will make or break you emotionally. If you can understand how to reframe the way you see things into a motivating, self-affirming direction, then you can achieve some of the most amazing goals and dreams in your life.

Realize you attract negative things into your life when you are not being true to your personal values. The negative things might come in the form of a person, which I find is typical, or a situation. The Universe has a way of maintaining its balance, and is pushing you to get back on your path, and back to the true you. For me, a good portion of my life was spent attracting chaotic relationships where I didn't own my power. Each relationship was trying to suck up 100 percent of my attention, leaving nothing left for me. In many of my relationships, I attracted people who didn't align with me in the area of health and fitness. My fitness routines of eating healthy and losing weight were threatening to them. Other boyfriends protested my spending my own money to advance my business and success. It made me second-guess who I was. As a result, my bank account would go down and my doubt would skyrocket.

I knew I had to take a good look at this pattern of chaos I kept attracting, so I would analyze each relationship to find how I was evoking the Law of Cause and Effect. But I couldn't really put it all together until I started understanding that I wasn't being true to who I was. I hired other coaches and relationship experts, who were very helpful in revealing to me what I couldn't see for myself. This is why getting coaching, mentoring, or reading a book like this is important if you keep attracting chaos into your life. Sometimes you need someone from the outside to show you your blind spots. The money I invested was well worth it because these coaches made me realize that there wasn't anything wrong with me—I was just settling for men who didn't appreciate my unique formula. They would instead try to project their own, often radically different, personal values onto me.

I remember once receiving a coaching session from a retired heart surgeon that went into Neuro-Lingistic Programming (NLP), and learned some great techniques on how to deal with a boyfriend at the time who had major anger issues. The doctor said something to me that made me shift my thinking. He told me that I was taking on my boyfriend's negative energy each time he got mad about what I perceived to be the stupidest things. Then there came a day when my boyfriend went off on me but I didn't take on his energy. I perceived that his anger wasn't about me, rather it was about his own unresolved issues. I went into my NLP mode of visualizing him as a small cartoon figure, which allowed me to completely change the way I was interpreting his angry ball of energy. I went into my office and let him have his little tantrum like a 3-year-old while I got some work done and enjoyed a bit of quiet time. This pattern continued for a while until one day I got wise and no longer felt like putting up with his behavior. Our relationship was going nowhere because we differed radically in our values. It was liberating when I was able to regain my power, get clear on my desires, and realize the relationship was a byproduct of my not valuing myself. That was why I had attracted this person into my life. Now I was ready for somebody better.

**Talk Like an Italian!**

Italian men and women both use their voices to express their truth. Many times while taking walks over the Ponte Vecchio bridge in Florence, Italy, I would overhear the animated conversations of people trying to get their points across. I guess I started to adsorb this mode of talking, because people would come up to me thinking that I was Italian and start conversing in the same way. I was soon able to carry on basic conversations, such as ordering my morning coffee, asking for directions, or even standing firm in my power when the unwanted attentions from men became too much!

### How Unconscious Motives Sabotage Your Goals and Desires

If you're not getting what you want and going to the next level of your life, ask yourself this question: "Where am I not valuing myself in my life?" I've worked with some very successful women from all walks of life, including CEOs, and I've encountered the same problems within all of them—they are not valuing themselves. As women, there are certain issues we tend to sweep under the rug. I say, don't sweep it under the rug. Bring those dust bunnies into your conscious mind and examine them. If you don't, unconscious motives will continue to sabotage your success.

What are unconscious motives and how do they impact achieving what you want in life? Unconscious motivation, or unconscious motives, refers to desires you possess that are hidden and unknown to you. These are the underlying factors that are sabotaging your success in any given area where you keep telling yourself you want to do something but end up doing the opposite.

Let's investigate a common example. Say you want to lose weight, yet you find yourself eating sugar and binging on food, even though consciously you know it's not what you really want to do. It's like someone else is taking over your body and making you eat those things. As a result, you start beating yourself up and thinking, Why can't I do what I say? How come I can't attract a better relationship, lose the weight, or do what my conscious mind desires? First, you must realize that the unconscious mind rules the show. In fact, if you have a fight between your conscious and unconscious minds, the unconscious will always win because it controls about 95 percent of your beliefs, habits, and behaviors. It's so powerful that when I work with clients on business, weight loss, relationships, or any goal they want to achieve, it's imperative we address the unconscious mind so that they can reprogram it for success. (Later in this book I'll teach you powerful techniques for changing your mental state and reprogramming your unconscious mind.)

This distinction between the conscious and unconscious minds is why just telling yourself on a conscious level that you want x, y, and z will not work! Your actions dictate your outcomes, and your actions emerge from your unconscious mind. Have you ever been driving to some familiar place—maybe work, the gym, or home—and when you arrive you don't remember the drive? It's because your unconscious mind took over your actions. Do you see how powerful it is? In fact, there's so much power in your unconscious mind, it's almost like you can go through your life on a daily basis and be in a hypnotic state. Imagine never having to will yourself to do something again: never diet again, never sabotage your efforts again. These things are possible if you know how your unconscious mind and unconscious motives work.

Earlier in the book I told you that years ago, while I was a fitness professional, I was in a negative relationship and found my unconscious motives taking over. One day I was feeling unhappy while on my way to train a client. Arriving early, I sat in the car and ate an entire box of protein bars. On highly emotional days like that, I would always resort to stuffing myself with food. Unsurprisingly, I gained weight, and then shamed myself for knowing better. Here I was, a fitness professional, and I couldn't get it together. On a conscious level, I of course knew overeating wasn't the right thing to do. But I felt out of control. Instead of addressing the situation on a conscious level, I was settling for the temporary "benefit" of gorging myself with food. Crazy, isn't it? Yes! But it shows just how powerful the unconscious mind is. Interestingly enough, as soon as I got the strength to leave that relationship the automatic bad eating habits disappeared. I didn't have to go to any therapy, either, I just followed my formula of being true to myself.

I've had some interesting relationships in my life, and each one has taught me a valuable lesson. Despite the drama, I actually learned a great deal about business from the relationship I just told you about. I looked at it as a lesson to stop settling, but to also learn how to hustle, sell, and learn the basics of business. I was crazy enough to move to Los Angeles from Ohio, not knowing a soul, and build my fitness business from scratch. I've had quite the journey and my motto has always been, "I don't want to live my life regretting not doing something." Even though some of my experiences taught me hard lessons, they were worth it because they helped mold the woman I am today, a catalyst and breakthrough specialist in developing human potential and shaping behaviors and habits. You meet people for a reason or a season, and whether it's a boyfriend, boss, friend, colleague, or client, you will always attract chaos when you are not being true to yourself. That's why it's wise to go after the challenges that inspire you and get you fired up, because if you don't, you'll be a magnet for turmoil.

I want you to explore the unconscious motives that currently are taking you away from an important goal. Let's say you want to get into better shape, yet your actions demonstrate movement toward the opposite goal. You find yourself eating sugar, skipping workouts, and doing other self-sabotaging things that take you further away from where you envision yourself. Or, maybe making more money is your current focus, yet you keep finding yourself doing things other than working on your business and following up with clients. Or, if you were like me, your goal is to stop dating men who are incongruent with your personal values.

Why is this happening? First, consider how these destructive behaviors might actually be providing you a benefit. I know that might sound counterintuitive, but you're actually getting something out of the chaos, something which stems from your unconscious motives. Let's explore the unconscious motives related to the fitness example. If you're eating sugar and can't stop, your body is feeding on the chemical addiction. When I am working with a client in this situation, I always ask them, "What's the benefit?" At first they might say something like, "Nothing. I just can't stop." I would then probe them about their life, specifically to determine what areas they are stressed about. If, for example, they tell me it's their relationship that's causing them stress, I can help them understand the "benefit" of their sugar consumption, namely that it helps them cope with their stress. If you're in the same boat, you're getting a dopamine fix from the sugar, which your unconscious mind is programmed to like.

From the example above, can you see how it's wise for you to examine the unwanted behaviors that are sabotaging your efforts to live a successful and fulfilling life? See if you can list the benefits you're getting out of your problematic behaviors. Put aside your emotions and try to see this exercise of self-examination as a scientific study of human behavior, with you as the subject of the experiment. In order to change, you have to bring forth your hidden motives into your conscious mind in order to become aware of them and change for the better. Try to seek linkages and connections, the way I came to realize how eating that entire box of protein bars gave me an immediate payoff which helped—for a short while at least—ease the pain of my relationship. Relieving stress on an animalistic level like that is perfectly normal. All I'm asking is that you try to become aware of what's compelling you to behave that way.

Of course, the real question is, even if you are aware of the linkage between your unconscious mind and your behaviors, how do you stop it? We will explore this question at end of this chapter, after we look at some of the ways in which you create obstacles for yourself that get you out of alignment and attract chaos. The more you can connect all these mental and emotional dots, the easier it will be for you to gain clarity on how to overcome even the most stubborn obstacles.

## What Happens When You're Not Crystal Clear on Your Desires

Let's return to the list of your top desires that we identified earlier in the book. Ask yourself two clarifying questions:

- What details am I leaving out?
- Where do I need to get clearer when stating my desires?

*"Create a clear vision so that your fear disappears."*

Right now, you're not living in alignment and being true to yourself. This means you might be throwing away your personal values and giving up on your dreams, which could be in the context of your relationships with your family or friends, or with your career, or with your health, or some other aspect of your life. If it feels like you've been saying YES to everyone except yourself and as a result feel "off," then you need to pay attention.

One or more of the seven areas of your life could be out of control. You will always attract someone or something to draw attention to your problems. Perhaps you are experiencing health issues? Your body is always providing feedback to your conscious mind about paying attention to and tackling the unresolved issues in your life. That feedback could be in the form of a cold, flu, or even cancer, each of which are wake-up calls for you to take back your power and focus on your goals. You owe it to yourself to love and honor what you desire and go after those things, no matter what. Don't reach the end of your life hoping and wishing you would have been or done more. Savor your life and stop settling for less.

## Chaos and Creation (Turning Obstacles into Opportunities)

Now that you know how and why you attract chaos into your life, you have the power to turn your biggest obstacles into opportunities. The possibilities are limitless. If you don't do this, you'll keep existing as the victim of your life instead of seizing victory. I've interviewed hundreds of successful entrepreneurs and leaders across the world, and a big part of their formula for creating massive success is learning how to overcome challenges. Each challenge they tackle gives them new perspective and broadens their horizon.

Imagine if you've never had a challenge in your entire life because you've always been sheltered, and then, all of the sudden, someone drops you off on a busy street corner in New York City where you have to fend for yourself. What would you do? Would you cave? Or would your survive and thrive? I've lived in New York City and I can honestly say it's a hard city to live in, but through my experiences there I was able to gain greater wisdom on navigating through chaos and challenges. I moved to New York right out of college, missing my graduation ceremony because I was so eager to tackle the Big Apple. I had a film internship and waited tables in one of the most frantic areas of Times Square. Working in a restaurant is a demanding job, and on top of that I had to deal with many rude and obnoxious people. On the plus side, I was able to meet plenty of celebrities, like Keanu Reeves (who is one of the coolest actors in Hollywood!), but I came to realize that this rat race type of life wasn't for me. Almost every night I cried because I didn't know a soul. But I was determined to figure things out. I knew I was tough and that this was all a big test for me.

So New York City was kicking my ass, and it felt like I was forcing everything instead of being in the flow. I was receiving signs from the Universe that made me realize that I didn't want to live there anymore, and that I didn't really want to pursue a film career. I'm not knocking the city itself, it just wasn't right for me. Some people love the energy of New York, but at that moment in my life it was out of alignment for me. The entire experience was tough, but it taught me how to survive on my own and finally freaking listen to my desires. The challenge taught me to answer important questions of what living my own La Dolce Vita Formula would look like. Isn't it interesting how you can go down one path in your life only to realize it's not you?

I haven't been back to New York City, but my experience there became incorporated into my life's formula by teaching me to be fearless in my pursuits. It also contributed another importance piece to my formula, my eventual mastery of fitness and health. It was while I was living there that I started to get into fitness and discovered that I had a love for working out. When I moved from New York City back to Ohio, I started to pursue the path of being a fitness professional. I went from wanting to be a film director to becoming a fitness fanatic. Go figure!

As I mentioned earlier, wherever your chaos lies, so do the challenges you must overcome. Your challenges are blessings from the Universe, and when you come to see them as such, your entire world will open up. It seems like my entire life, from as early as I can remember, has been a set of challenges that I had to learn to overcome—everything from my learning disorder, being bullied, not feeling good enough, attracting crappy relationships, being overweight, repeatedly sabotaging my own progress, and money issues.

Can you relate to any or maybe all of these things? If so, know that I've put my heart and soul into helping women just like you. And I'm so very glad we're partners. I know you have what it takes to go to the next level, but sometimes you get in your own way, just as I so frequently did in my own life. But I don't care how smart you are or what has or hasn't happened in your life. I want you to realize one simple thing: you can change anything you want. If you can realize that, then you'll grow as a person and come to relish the inevitable challenges that come your way because you'll understand that facing challenges is how you grow.

I want you to look back at your life and connect the dots, and see how each challenge has created your unique formula. You are the woman you are today because of those experiences. Even if you're going through something tough right now, it's okay because you can transform and transcend those challenges that are holding you hostage. Let me show you how to gain back your power. Let's turn those obstacles into opportunities!

First, take a look at the number one thing that you feel is keeping you stuck. Maybe it's money, and that no matter what you do, you keep getting hit by unexpected bills. Maybe you've lost your job and feel purposeless. Look at the challenge, whatever it may be, and ask yourself, How is going through this a benefit to me? At first you might not see the benefits, but trust me, they are there.

Here's a brief story that may help you with this exercise. I was once working with a client who was going through a divorce. She got stuck with all of the bills, so I asked her, "How is this a benefit?" She paused, and then started to go off on her ex. So I asked the question a different way: "How is having to take on the responsibility of paying bills a benefit to you growing your business and raising your children?" Since I knew her highest personal values were related to her business and her children, this question started to change her perception. I kept asking her what another benefit was, and then other one, until she could see the value this great challenge could bring to her life. The act of processing my probing questions helped her to balance out her mind.

When you have an imbalanced mind, you're not likely to take the best actions. That's why it's important to always ask yourself these often difficult questions in order to get your mental state in order. Always strive for greater self-awareness. I know sometimes this hard thinking can feel challenging, but there are serious drawbacks if you don't do it. The most obvious drawback is that you will stay exactly where you're at, feeling stuck and victimized, and not living your desires and dreams. You must ask enough questions—and keep asking them—to discover the benefits to be gained from your current situation. With these insights, you can shift internally. So I want you to go deep and ask yourself empowering questions about all areas of your life.

**How is {INSERT YOUR CHALLENGE HERE} a benefit to me in every area of life?**

As a quick reminder, the areas of your life can be broken up into seven categories:

1. Life Purpose
2. Family/Relationship
3. Friends
4. Finances
5. Fitness
6. Mindset
7. Vocation/Career/Business

Every obstacle you face provides a benefit to one or more of the areas of life, and if you can't find the benefit it that tells me you're not wanting to shift. Perhaps you're not yet ready. Yes, this process can be challenging, but it is also liberating because right from the start it changes the way you think about any situation. Imagine if you learned how to rewire your brain the moment you perceived a challenge by asking yourself, What is the benefit? This technique's power stems in part from that fact that it forces you to stop giving yourself a pity party and repeatedly sharing your sad tale with others. I know as women we like to talk, but it doesn't help to retell the same story over and over again, expecting yourself to think and act differently by doing so. From my experience, if you keep focusing on what is not working, your mind can't find a way to solve your problems. Also, once you have seen the benefits your difficulties are actually giving you, you can start focusing on how you can turn these things into opportunities.

Recently, one of my clients appeared on TV, and she was fuming because they had strict policies for controlling her appearance and told her to not say this or say that. I first told her that's the way the media works, and you have to follow their rules if you want to be on TV, but I also let her know that I got that she felt her brand wasn't being represented in the way she felt was in alignment with her values. Instead of saying, "I'm so sorry that happened," I said something that would give her power back: "How is what happened to you a benefit?" She was able to quickly shift mental gears and tell me. You might be thinking I am a hard cookie and not compassionate by giving her that response, but that couldn't be further from the truth because this client is owning her power and doing amazing things in her business and life.

No one said it would be easy to live your truth and own your power. I love working with women who seek to push the limits of what they can do. I am the person to get them there, and it's through tough love. Some of the best mentors I've had in my life have demonstrated this by always kicking me out of my pity parties and shifting me into prosperity thinking. To me, this approach is the only way I can help someone get out of their way and live their highest potential.

Just like Einstein said, you can't solve a problem in the same mind in which it was created. What this means is that you have to change the way that you are looking at your situation. You actually want to take on challenges in your life that are inspiring, because you actually make your brain smarter that way. You grow you brain.

**A Recipe for Awakening Your Unique Abilities**

Neuroscientist Marian Diamond (who recently died at the age of 90) studied Einstein's brain for years. At first her findings showed that his brain had the same amount of neurons as an average person's brain. Later, she discovered Einstein possessed for more glial cells than most people ("glial" means glue in Greek). This is important for you to know because the more you increase the amount of glial cells in your brain, the more you will be thinking like a fearless female (and maybe a bit more like Einstein, too!).

When I work with clients, I have a specific process where I show clients how to produce more glial cells to awaken their unique abilities. When you do this, you will birth new ideas, create more impact, and your income will increase as a result. It's scientifically proven and predictable, and it's like following a recipe. Marian Diamond's research showed that there are five things Einstein did to increase the amount of glial cells in his brain: maintain a good diet, get sufficient exercise, challenge yourself, embrace novelty, and love. You can do the same things! Now I'm going to reformulate that list into the seven areas of focus I believe you need to engage in to maximize your La Dolce Vita Formula for fabulous living:

**1. & 2. Have a proper diet and exercise routine**

As an ambitious woman, it's critical for you to take care of yourself and create a plan for optimum heath. Why? Because your health is your wealth! Years ago I ran a fitness business, and I realized after winning the Ms. Midwest States Natural body building contest that my mind led me to win. You see, I had tried many diets before and kept failing because I wasn't uncovering the real secret to creating my ideal body. Once I put my mind right, my body followed. Now I look back on those miserable, unhealthy years and view them as an important part of my journey toward life mastery.

**3. Take on challenges!**

It's true what they say: use it or lose it. Maximum growth in biology happens on the brink of stability and challenge. If you want your life to change you have to realize that it will require you to take on bigger things. You have to invest in yourself—with time and money—and understand that taking calculated risks is necessary. Every driven woman knows this and intuitively understands that to jump to the next level of her life she needs to go after challenges that inspire her. Stretch yourself out of your comfort zone, because to live full out you need to stop playing it safe.

**4. Create new patterns. Stop doing the same routine and mix things up.**

We all get into the habit of doing the same things over and over because those things lie within our comfort zone. But this repeating pattern stagnates the brain. It's only when you mix things up or change the way you do things that you can birth ingenious ideas. Find new ways to optimize all parts of your life, from your daily routines to your daily strategies!

Think about your morning routine, maybe one day you meditate on the beach and the next day you workout at the gym, listening to your favorite podcast. One of the things I recommend you do is to look at one goal that you want to master and keep asking yourself the question, "How can I make this better?" You might try to cut down the time it takes, or find a more efficient way to perform a routine task.

**5. Learn and master things outside of your normal skill set.**

Empowered women emerge from new ideas and skills sets that at first can feel awkward or difficult. Think about an area you are a master in. Did you always feels as confident as you do now? Seek to encourage your brain to grow by learning new skills, even if they are unrelated to your goal. For example, I took up ballroom dancing to help my brain rewire and be more in the flow. At first I felt frustrated because everyone else seemed to be a pro and I felt like I had two left feet. After I started to master the basic steps, my confidence went up and I began to tap into creative juices for other projects. In fact, in one of my shows you will see me swing dancing in front of everyone to a choreographed number I created with a seasoned pro.

**6. Love**

You must love all parts of you, even your past. If you don't, then you won't open up to receive new ideas, reach your goals, and attract amazing opportunities. Strive to embrace all parts of yourself, the good and the bad. This is an important part of your spiritual growth for you to master, because if you don't you'll keep rerunning in your mind the stories that keep you stuck. Help this process along by going back into your life, trace every trauma, and turn it into a transformative realization that all of those events were necessary for your growth.

**7. Find the formula that makes you fabulous**

What is the most unique thing about yourself that no one else has?

The quality of your life is greatly determined by asking yourself quality questions like that one. Start asking better questions and you can transform problems into opportunities. If you're not sure how to start, begin by asking questions that satisfy your curiosity. The polymath Leonardo da Vinci, perhaps best know the painting the Mona Lisa, was curious about a great many things. He formed the habit of writing down any question he had about a problem or concept he wanted to figure out. Then he kept writing the same question. He understood the power of repetition: if you keep asking the question, your brain will sync up to the Universe and you'll find the answers you're seeking. The solutions will appear when you *keep* asking.

Try it! Set a timer for an hour and repeatedly ask the question that you want an answer to. Feel free to reformulate the question as you go through the exercise, and see what shows up as a result. An answer might come forth during the exercise, or it might appear in other ways, such as through an email subject line, an overheard conversation at Starbucks, or somewhere else. The key is to be patient and expect the answers to come, because they most certainly will, although sometimes it takes a bit of time.

I've seen how CEOs and other very sharp people I work with refuse to let problems get the best of them. They simply get quiet and ask empowering questions. It might take you a few days, weeks, maybe even a month to find answers to some of your questions. Don't pressure yourself. This exercise is a lesson in being able to change the way you see and solve problems.

I know sometimes things can feel heavy, and I don't want you to negate your feelings, as they are powerful forces in guiding you to your goals and vision. In fact, I encourage you to use your feelings; feel what you need to feel, but don't stay in a negative state because it will paralyze you emotionally, physically, and mentally. When you're stuck or frustrated, it's best to do something that's nurturing. For example, if I have a problem I feel I can't solve in the moment, I will talk to a friend, my boyfriend, or anyone else I feel I can trust, just to get it out of my system. I am not necessarily looking for guidance, as sometimes a girl just needs to vent. Then, I will go to my favorite Starbucks and treat myself to Clover coffee and read or write in my journal. I will share with you in the chapter "Changing Your Mental State" some powerful strategies that will help you in overcoming challenges and problem solving.

### Finding Viable Solutions to Replace Bad Habits

Are you stuck in a rut of trying to break a bad habit? Are you saying you want one thing but your body is doing another? When I have clients who want to break bad habits, but whose actions aren't congruent with what they are telling me they want, I know their unconscious is running the show, unaligned with their conscious desires. I mentioned earlier the incident when I ate an entire box of protein bars, and how I would binge on pizza and junk food, even though consciously I knew those were self-sabotaging behaviors. Clearly my unconscious mind was dictating the terms of my life.

Earlier in the chapter I mentioned that I would teach you how to break your bad habits and your self-sabotaging ways, so let's get started. Go ahead and list all of the benefits you are getting from overeating, spending money like an addict, and getting yourself in the bad-boy relationships (or not even putting yourself out there). Again, the central question to ask is, what are you doing that doesn't align with what you say you want? The problem lies in those areas.

For example, lets go back to the bad behavior of eating sugar and say your goal is to drop fifteen pounds of fat. My question to you is, "What's the payoff for eating that sugar?" This questions speaks to where the unconscious motives are kicking in, and why you need to be able to uncover the benefits you are getting so that you can change the outcome. In this case, you are eating the sugar because you're stressed. The benefit is that you get a dopamine fix. Another payoff is that you don't have to address the root reasons for your stress. Maybe you're afraid if you get in shape that your partner will hurt you emotionally. That's why you always see in the movies or commercials women running for tubs of ice cream to soothe their emotions. I used to be one of those women, but today I don't do that because I've learned how to break those self-sabotaging patterns. In fact, it's so ingrained in me that I don't have to think about it, meaning that I'm on "automatic" because my unconscious mind now powers *good* decision-making, and my conscious mind doesn't even have to get involved. What I do instead is read, watch something that is funny, go for a walk, workout, talk to a friend, journal, meditate, or take on a creative project. You name the former bad habit, I have replaced it with an alternative.

This is where must really search your awareness and list as many of the payoffs you are getting from your bad behaviors as you can, because understanding this is how you can overcome your hurdles. If you create a good, honest questions list, you can't help but see how doing x (the self-sabotaging behavior) takes you away from your goal.

After creating your list of benefits, next create a list of alternative actions that you could be doing instead, along the lines of the alternatives I listed above that I use. Then ask yourself how doing those specific alternative things will help you to reach your goals. Keep asking yourself that question until your brain is wired and fired to take the action. Repetition is the key to reprogramming your mind for success. Do it over and over until you, too, are on automatic.

*"Rock bottom became the solid foundation on which I rebuilt my life."*
*—J.K. Rowling*

**Fearless and Fabulous Female Profile**

**Elena Cornaro Piscopie** (1646–1684) was the daughter of an important Venetian nobleman. When her father recognized how skilled she was, he arranged for her to study Greek, Latin, Jewish, Spanish, philosophy, and theology. When Elena was 32, she became the first woman in history to graduate from the University of Padua, one of the most important seventeenth century centers of learning. She was awarded a degree in philosophy (she couldn't receive a theology degree because she was a woman).

Envision yourself breaking through your own limitations, just like Elena did. She was a woman who passionately believed in her mission of self-education. In order to align yourself with your desires you must be able to overcome challenges and dedicate yourself to pursuing what's most inspiring to you. Anytime you feel like stopping, think about Elena and how much opposition she faced. You're no different than her. Embrace her fearlessness and see yourself as the same powerful force.

### Chapter Summary

Chapters One and Two helped you to get clear on what's important in your life so you could better understand what goals you should pursue. That's a big part of the La Dolce Vita Formula, but there's another important task before you which this chapter helped you tackle: uncovering the obstacles in your way, particularly the unconscious motives that cause you to self-sabotage your plans and that keep you stuck.

Learning how to bring these invisible roadblocks into your conscious mind will make you aware of them, which is the first step toward changing your mindset so you can create the success you desire. Moreover, you can come to view these setbacks as being benefits, and can use them as tools to inspire mental shifts that help you find solutions quickly. When you understand that challenges are actually blessings in disguise, you will move ever more quickly toward living a fabulous life.

# Part Two
# How to Master Your Mind to Achieve Your Goals

# "Success Starts in Your Mind First"

# CHAPTER FOUR
# CHANGING YOUR MENTAL STATE

*"Life shrinks or expands in proportion to one's courage" —Anais Nin*

Just to recap, in the previous chapters you learned who you really are by understanding your unique La Dolce Vita Formula, which is based on your personal values, and you got clear on your desires and the goals you want to set. I also shared how to uncover and overcome the self-sabotaging behaviors and unconscious motives that are setting you back. You now have the tools to turn your challenges into opportunities. If you feel stuck on any of these points, go back and reread those chapters, as you'll want to make sure you have these formulas firmly in place.

This chapter is about transforming your mindset. My knowledge about mindset is one of the most inspiring things for me to share with my readers and clients, because I love to see the amazing changes this information can bring to people's lives. You've already learned that your unconscious mind is responsible for around 95 percent of your beliefs, habits, and behaviors. This is the reason why I like to focus on mental state first before creating any kind of strategy for goal-setting. The path to success begins in your mind. You must change your self-image in order to change your outer world. In his book *Psycho-Cybernetics*, Dr. Maxwell Maltz introduced the concept that a person must have an accurate and positive view of him- or herself before setting goals; otherwise, he or she will get stuck in a continuing pattern of limiting beliefs. Maltz's ideas focus on visualizing one's goals, because he believes that self-image is the cornerstone of all the changes that take place in a person. According to Maltz, if one's self-image is unhealthy or faulty, all of his or her efforts will end in failure.

I've related previously how I once had a poor self-image of my body; no matter what diet I tried, I couldn't get myself into the shape I wanted to be in. That didn't change until, finally, my self-image changed. Do you remember the movie *The Terminator*? There is a scene in the movie where the character Sarah Connor, played by Lynda Hamilton, was doing pull ups. I recall watching that scene in awe of her buff physique—to me, hers was my ideal body that I visualized for myself. So my mental state concerning my physique changed, which gave me fuel to recreate my body from the inside out. I would go into the gym every day and visualize myself looking like Sarah during my workout. I never missed a workout, either, because I was inspired to transform my body. I kept this goal a secret and told no one of what I was doing. No one knew about the images playing on the movie screen of my mind.

A few months later, after lots of hard work, I would have the amazing experience of complete strangers coming up to me and saying, "You know who you look like? You look like Lynda Hamilton from *The Terminator*." My heart skipped a beat every time this happened, because I still didn't fully appreciate the power of my mind. I knew what I was doing in terms of my actions, but at the time I didn't connect the dots and realize that it was the *inner* work of visualizing the body I wanted that was truly responsible for those actions, the actions that ultimately created the outer world of my actually having that fit and athletic body. It wasn't until years later that I finally grasped this and understood the power of mental state. Once I did, I used that knowledge to create a fitness system that taught other women how to use their minds to create their ideal bodies.

I related this story because I want you to realize that the mental mechanism that help me also exists inside you. You, too, can create the reality you want. Our personal reality exists in the things we visualize in our mind, which means you must be able to put yourself in a mental state that is in alignment with your values and goals. This takes practice! Everyday, I would focus on changing my mental state to create my ideal body. Since I had the desire to change my body—something that my personal values were urging me to do—it felt like I was in the flow instead of needing to force things to happen.

That's why it's wise to occasionally check in with yourself to see if what you are saying you want is actually in alignment with your highest values. As discussed earlier in the book, ask yourself questions to figure out if your actions are matching your true desires. If they are not, you'll find yourself feeling frustrated because you're out of sync with your true self. Now, it goes without saying that part of having a good mental state is to visualize realistic expectations. Having unrealistic expectations of yourself is a recipe for disaster. Want to lose fifteen pounds of fat in one week? Sorry, but that's an unrealistic expectation that will set you up for failure and crush your soul. Slow and steady wins the race.

Later in this chapter you will learn how to shift your mental state by using your senses, but first let's examine what your current beliefs and perceptions are with regard to your desires and goals. Do you hold any beliefs that are causing you friction in your life? If so, we must shift the way you perceive things on the mental plane. This technique is how you can get yourself into the flow and start consistently taking action to achieve your goals. That path leads to success, and is far easier and less stressful than trying to force things to happen.

We can tie into the mindset of the barista and how they trained themselves mentally to master the art of a perfect cup of coffee. Since they've dedicated hours or training to their craft every movement is unconscious because they don't think, they just do. They pride themselves on mastery and the Italian way of not deviating from what they feel is perfection.

**The Barista Mindset**

The art of making a perfect cup of coffee is taken very seriously in Italy, where being a barista is considered a profession. Baristas there master coffee-making and coffee service (dedicating countless hours to training in their craft), and treat the entire operation as an art form, from the way they ground the beans to how they serve the beverage. Italians serve coffee in smaller sizes—no Starbucks venti-size cups there!—and focus with extreme detail on every aspect of the service. To a barista, preparing and serving a cup of coffee is something of a heroic effort, and they do it with passion and seriousness. Furthermore, their mental training allows their most every movement to be done without conscious effort or thought.

### The Current Formula of Your Beliefs and Perceptions

Beliefs are like the glue that keeps mind and body functioning together in harmony. They greatly assist you in achieving your goals, so it's important to understand what's going on inside of your mind. You can create beliefs that stick and support you in being successful, or you can hold onto ones that sabotage and limit you, with the result being you don't take action.

First, let's examine those beliefs that are getting in your way. I want you to ask yourself a simple question: "What things am I putting in my own way that are blocking me from success in having x or accomplishing y?" Scan your mind honestly, and I'm guessing it won't take you long at all to know what the problem is. I've asked this question to women all over the world and it's always a variation of the same thing: it's easy for you to keep reinforcing your fears, and as a result you stay put exactly where you're at. So fear is, for most women, the underlying culprit and mental block. That's why it's so important to identify your specific fears in order to change your mental state.

Below is a list of the familiar fears that I hear about all the time. I want you to write down or circle which fears you can identify with the most:

- Fear of not being smart enough
- Fear of authority figures
- Fear of success
- Fear of failure/loss
- Fear of approval
- Fear of not being pretty enough
- Fear of not having enough vitality and health
- Fear of losing loved ones

*"Whatever you fear will appear."*

There's no such thing as fear of the unknown, by the way, because there's always content to what your fear is dictating. Typically people will allow past events to reinforce their fears. Conversely, fear can also be a good thing because it can stop you from doing something that is not in alignment with who you are. It's important to know if the fear you are running away from or that is stopping you is just a story that you can break through. If you know it's just a story you repeatedly tell yourself, then you must take the time to work through the fear and learn how to dissolve it.

Imagine being able to rewrite the story of your biggest fears so that you dissolve them. You can do that by first figuring out if the block you wish to break through is preventing you from being aligned with your highest personal values. If it is, then take a moment to reflect on how being able to dissolve this fear will empower you in every area of your life, because you'll be back in tune with your values. Go down the list of the seven areas, and ask yourself the following questions:

"How will breaking through my fear of x help me in the area of . . .

- my finances
- my life's purpose
- my family/relationship
- my career/business

- my fitness/health
- my mindset
- my social influence

The more benefits you can come up with through this exercise, the easier it is to shift your mindset and conquer your inner critic. At all times, keep in the forefront of your mind the belief that this is your life, and if you give it away trying to please others and not going after your own dreams, you'll live a small, unsatisfying existence.

Do you remember my story about my investing in that first mentor? I had spread out all of my credit cards and knew I had enough money to afford one payment toward the coaching. I experienced a moment of fear—in fact, it I was terrified about taking the action. I immediately thought, *What happens if this doesn't work?* I was fearful of repeating the same mistakes that had happened before. I didn't want to fail again, nor did I want to lose more money.

What spurred me to action was this desperate feeling that I didn't have a choice. I had to do something! I was sick of my negative beliefs around money and was ready to take a leap of faith to change my life. I knew that my goals and desires were in alignment, and I had no distractions, no crazy men in my life to mess things up. I knew the time for action was now.

This is why investing in yourself is always a personal choice. When I have potential clients who are considering whether or not to work with me, I tell them that working with me is an investment, and in order to get results you have to be all in. There's no dipping your toe in the water, either; you just jump right in and take the plunge. It's okay that there might be a little fear when we start; in fact, it's a good thing, because it presents me the opportunity to coach them to change the way they are looking at fear. I encourage you to do the same things.

**Fearless and Fabulous Female Profile**

**Florence Nightingale** (1820–1910) was born in Florence, Italy, on May 12, 1820. She grew up feeling socially awkward; however she was passionate about philanthropic pursuits. Nightingale eventually came to the conclusion that nursing was her calling; in fact, she believed the vocation to be her divine purpose. When she told her parents that she wanted to pursue nursing, they were opposed and forbade her to do it. That didn't stop her because her desire was so strong she was able to break through the fear of her parents' and society's disapproval to go after her dreams.

Nightingale is now seen as a pioneer in the field of nursing due to her actions during the Crimean War. The ill and injured soldiers during that war suffered an atrocious lack of care because the military hospitals were understaffed and unsanitary. By request of Secretary of War Sidney Herbert, Nightingale gathered a group of nurses to help the sick and dying. People referred to her as the Lady with the Lamp. Others simply called her the Angel of the Crimea. Her work reduced the hospital's death rate by two-thirds.

Think about what you are fearing the most and see yourself having the same kind of strength as Florence Nightingale. She had a burning desire to go after her dreams, and refused to let her parents or society dictate her destiny. As a modern day woman, can you trace back in your life to a time when you held fast and owned your power? Do you see the challenges you've overcome, and how they've made you who you are today?

Let's take a look at a situation from your past which you have labeled as bad, something you know is still holding you back from achieving what you want. Think of something that is creating a self-sabotaging pattern that has sapped your ability to take action. Take yourself back to that bad situation and try to recall what you were feeling in the moment. Add details: Where were you? What people were with you? What year was it, what season, what time of day? Get your visualization as specific as you can so you replay the event on the movie screen of your mind. Then I want you to observe yourself as if you are two people in that situation. One person is the past you from that time, and the other is you as you are now, witnessing the situation as it's happening. What are you perceiving as you do this exercise? Are you feeling anxious? Are you feeling frightened?

What's going on in that moment is you are *creating* memories through your perception of the past event. Your perception of how you see the situation can debilitate you and cause an imbalance that literally wires your brain to lock in that limiting belief system. Perceptions are created through your senses (which is why I asked you to add sensory details to your visualization), and can actually cause disease in the body, something studied by the field of epigenetics.

I've seen this demonstrated quite powerfully by a friend I had who would trigger a migraine each time she wasn't valuing herself. It was fascinating watching each episode play out with the same results. She would start dating a guy and get infatuated with him. But the moment she perceived that he (inevitably) didn't measure up to her standards, like clockwork her body would trigger a migraine. I kept telling her that there was a connection between her migraines and the stress from her relationships, but she didn't want to listen and kept playing out her story about how she was a victim. Our relationship ended because I could no longer enable her. She literally made herself sick, stopped working on herself and her business altogether, and lost her house. I couldn't get her to understand that she was doing this to herself. I tried to spell it out many times, but every time I would tell her what was going on, she didn't want to listen to me and threw a tantrum. This friendship became a drain on my psyche and I had to let it go. I was honest with her and let her know that I could no longer support her self-destructive ways.

**Epigenetics and You**

For years I've been fascinated by how perceptions are linked to epigenetics. I've interviewed and trained with some of the world's leading authorities on the subject, like Dr. Bruce Lipton, and have come to appreciate just how powerful an effect perceptions can have on the body. If you're interested, here are some details on the connection.

Epigenetics is essentially the study of the switches that turn our gene expression on and off. Our environment can promote this on/off gene expression process, but what's really interesting is the correlation researchers have uncovered between *psychology* and physiology impacting the genes. For example, lets say you perceive something as bad through the lens of your personal values, such as a client or boss telling you that you've made a mistake by yelling at you. If you lack the self-awareness to consciously process what's happening in the moment, you will internalize the event as a traumatic experience, which means you will unconsciously file that memory into your cell tissues. If that memory is "charged" with enough negative emotion, it can cause diseases, such as cancer, autoimmune diseases, and sickness in general.

The website WhatIsEpigenetics.com uses a very helpful analogy to help people better understand epigenetics. They liken the human lifespan to a very long movie, with DNA providing the instructions, or script. Epigenetics, then, would play the role of director, taking the formal script and tweaking it, for better or worse, to suit his desires.

As you can see, I believe it's important for you to have at least a very basic understanding of epigenetics and of how your perceptions impact your nervous system and, ultimately, your health. Your mind really is your center of power. When you perceive something to be stressful, your nervous system is triggered, which it affects your body on a cellular level.

Can you see now how you create your internal world through your perceptions? You can look at a situation and label it bad because it challenges your personal values, or you can see the exact same situation and perceive it as something good that supports your personal values. We are constantly filtering our reality through our value system, with every incident we experience and each person we meet. We reflexively see people as being good because they support us or bad because they are challenging us. What if I told you that both the good and the bad were necessary for your personal evolution? That both are essential parts of your formula for living a fulfilling life and getting to the next level?

The nervous system is the master controller of the body, and know that will leave you better prepared to meet challenges. If, for example, you're in a negative state due to the way you perceive a certain situation, you'll be charged with emotion, and this will impact your cell physiology and create stress. But *knowing* the mechanics for why this is happening can open up the door toward a different, more empowering perception. You can then take control of the situation and reframe it to your advantage.

When I am working with a client who all of the sudden gets sick, I ask them if they are following their truth. I ask, "Where are you giving your power away, because right now I can see that your body is trying to get the attention of your conscious mind?" It usually turns out that they are not paying enough attention to their health, so they never fully relax and let go of their stress.. Another frequent culprit for their physical ailment is that they spend too much time saying "Yes" to everyone in their life except for themselves, so now they are out of alignment.

Years ago, I used to get chronic bladder infections, so I went to several western medical doctors. They all wanted to get me to take antibiotics, which in my value system is a huge no-no. I remember the day one doctor told me I had to be on antibiotics for the rest of my life. This was before I was studying epigenetics and specific types of illnesses, but still I knew there was no way I was going to listen to this doctor. I was going to take a holistic approach to heal my body because I intuitively knew that's what my body needed. I would find the answers myself.

I left the doctors behind and started to read the literature on the mind-body connection. This knowledge help steer me to get out of the relationships that were toxic to my soul. As a result, my body started to heal. Once I started to follow my unique La Dolce Vita Formula for what made me happy, my body responded. I also threw away those damn pills and haven't been to a doctor since for that problem. You might guess that I have a love-hate relationship with medical doctors. Yes, there are some amazing ones out there who truly seek to help their patients, but then there are ones—usually operating out of ignorance—for whom the entire discussion of the mind-body connection is a nonstarter. They would rather get you hooked on pills instead of looking at root causes.

Think what we could do if we were to focus more on changing a sick person's mental state naturally instead of shoving pills down their throat. The opioid epidemic is crazy and yet there's nothing substantial I see being done about it. Why is that? It's because the drug companies are in business to make money, and therefore, in my opinion, healthcare is not about getting you healthy, it's about keeping you just on the edge of functioning. If you want wellness and you want to save on your health insurance, then invest your time and energy in changing your mental state. It's the best medicine. I have helped my clients to take charge of their health and create wellness by empowering them mentally and helping them live their truth.

Don't get me wrong: I have respect for many doctors, but not for the ones who are promoting prescription medications without also addressing the most fundamental causes of illness. I think now more than ever people are starting to wake up to this, or at least I hope they are. I will of course go to the doctor if I break an arm or need urgent care, but when I am feeling under the weather I ask myself a more empowering question: "Where am I not being true to myself? In what area in my life am I really off balance?" Within a few seconds of asking myself these questions, I can pinpoint the problem.

I encourage you to be proactive about your health because it is your wealth. If you don't have your health, money and everything else in your life doesn't matter. I am not dispensing medical advice here, either; I am just sharing my personal philosophy, values, and experience. To expand on how your perceptions shape your beliefs, Dr. Joe Dispenza, author of the book *You Are the Placebo*, explains the neuroscience behind taking medication and why we form the beliefs we hold around medicine. Dr. Dispenza writes about the fundamental question of how medication, your health, and your mental state are all tied together. Have you ever asked yourself, after taking an aspirin, whether it's the aspirin that's actually helping the headache, or your *belief* that the aspirin is working? There's so much controversy around this subject. However, if you are reading this book, you have an open mind and are willing to explore all sides of an issue.

One of the reasons I've looked deeply into this subject is because of my past own health concerns. I wanted to understand the truth of how we create disease and illness in our bodies. I also wanted to better understand the relationship between the unconscious and conscious minds, which of course ties into our goals and desires. My research showed how powerful our beliefs are; you can create or destroy your life through the power of your mind. This is why the best prescription you can give yourself is to master your thoughts, perceptions, and emotions.

The decisions you make must be rooted in what you believe is best for you. So many times in your life, you've been told what to think, so challenge your beliefs on every level and area of your life and identify patterns of thought that aren't consistent with your true self. It's interesting that we can see this process take place on a much larger, global scale. Consider how once we believed the world was flat. People were burned at the stake for holding beliefs about the world that were different from the common wisdom. But, slowly and surely, humanity's belief in a flat earth shifted because it was simply incongruent with what we came to understand about our world.

Imagine being able to shift your perceptions about your own inner world. What would it do for you if you could positively re-envision your internal image of yourself and took action so that your outer world reflected that vision? This is exactly what I am pushing you toward. I want you to realize that you create your reality through your innermost dominant thoughts and feelings. Seize this powerful knowledge! Understand that your dominant thoughts and feelings are either nudging you to take positive, life-changing action, or they are keeping your inert and unhappy because they limit your belief of what is possible in your life. Whatever you believe you will perceive. I like to think that you, the conscious and ambitious woman, is waking up to her greatness and highest potential.

*"We should never wait for science to give us permission to do the uncommon." —Dr. Joe Dispenza,*

### Take Inventory of Your Beliefs

Right now I want you to take inventory of your beliefs, both the ones that are supporting you and the ones that are not. For example, let's say one of your goals is to make more money, but you harbor a belief that making money is hard. No matter what you do, it always seems like an uphill battle. Or perhaps you've wanted to get into shape and each time you attempt to do so you keep failing because you think you have to struggle to make progress. You've been told because you're older that it's really hard to get fit, and you've bought into that belief. For each belief you identify, ask yourself these questions:

- Why do I believe this?
- How or where did I learn this belief, or who gave it to me it?

Question and scrutinize each and every belief in order to determine if it is supporting you or working against you. My second question, above, emphasizes finding the sources of your beliefs. Finding the source where a belief originated from will give you additional context and information, which in turn will empower you to change the belief patterns that are holding you back. For example, maybe you want to make more money but you grew up in a family where money was seen as bad, evil, and hard to acquire. So your belief about money originated in childhood, where it took hold because of your perception of your parents' financial struggles. This context can help you understand that your limiting beliefs stem from a time long past, and don't necessarily pertain at all to your situation today. That's why it's wise to understand *why* you believe what you believe. Get to the root of it, and don't blame your parents for signaling a bad belief to you; after all, it's the program they were given, too, when they were young.

In this example, you need to break the paradigm by changing your perceptions and beliefs about money. Since the brain is neuroplastic (meaning you are not hard-wired; you can change the way you perceive things), you can literally in seconds change this pattern by retraining your brain, if you know the right questions to ask. The reason why it is hard for most people to do this is that they are simply asking the wrong questions, such as, "Why am I so broke? Why can't I get it together?" These disempowering questions create a feedback loop to your unconscious mind, saying, "Yeah, you're right. Okay, we will keep reinforcing this!" Later on I will talk about how your words have tremendous power in controlling your mental state, and that you have control over them, as well.

Now let's go to the next step. I want you to think about the limiting perceptions you hold of the events in your life, from the distant past up until right now, and consider how you could change the way you see those event by being able to balance out your mind. You can do this by asking yourself, *What is the benefit to me that I experienced from this?* The challenging part is that you might say, "Heather, so and so did this to me and there's no benefit!" But I ask you to look again and keep asking the question, because there's always a benefit. Many times we don't see it because we are mentally imbalanced in this area, blinded because we cling to the perceptions that support us in being a victim, instead of changing out those beliefs for ones that help to empower us to move on. The sad story you keep telling yourself won't free your mind from what is holding you back; it can only block you from achieving what you really want out of life.

I've worked with women from all walks of life, and I've taken some of them from intense, very difficult situations to new places where they were able to free themselves mentally and change the way they perceived their situations. They were able to connect the dots in their life and realize that their life's purpose or spiritual awakening was always there in the background, trying to guide them to be so much more. We all have stories we tell ourselves about our lives; it's how we leverage those stories to inspire and guide us that gets us to where we want to go. That's' why I've been sharing with you my stories of being disempowered in all areas of my life, because who would I be without my stories? Now I am the woman who helps other women, just like you, break through their self-sabotaging stories, get inspired by their empowering stories, and go on to achieve amazing things. Simply stated, to go and live your fearless, fabulous La Dolce Vita life.

To me, that's what the game of life is all about. There will always be other levels to conquer within yourself, if you're willing and ready to do the inner work. If not, then you'll live a life where you feel you're forever settling for something mediocre. Is that really who you are? I know it's not, because something compelled you to read this book. You want me to call you out on your B.S. and prod you to take action. And I am here to do just that for you.

I once worked with a client, also a fitness professional like me, who was trying to wrap her mind around why she had gained a lot of weight and was feeling miserable. I immediately knew my first job was to help her shift her mental state, so I asked her what benefits she gained by having the extra weight? She was able to rattle off over twenty benefits, among them that the extra weight made her stop dating jerks and allowed her to eat what she wanted. She knew her weight problem showed her clients that she was human, too, but she realized that she didn't want to eat mindlessly anymore. If she could break through this issue, it would demonstrate for her clients that they could do the same. I can relate because, as I've described, I went through this same dilemma myself.

The key is to not beat yourself up over whatever you've done or not done. You're at the starting point, and the goal now is to neutralize your negative perceptions and start looking at the benefits of your current behavior. We talked about how there's always a benefit and drawback happening at the same time, it's just that our minds are wired to see only what we want through our own personal values.

If you are a mother and you see someone verbally harassing your child, you will automatically perceive that person to be bad since it goes against your values of loving and caring for your child. What if you were to see the actual benefit of that situation? I know you are thinking there's no way someone calling your child names could possibly be a benefit. But what if through that experience there was a benefit, namely that you stood up for not only yourself, but for your child, too? What if your actions taught your child the valuable lesson that they need to stand up for themselves? Maybe your child has always seen you as the mousy, submissive one, but lost that perception forever after observing how you took a stand against a bully. Wouldn't that be quite a benefit? It could be, if you simply open your mind enough to perceive it that way.

Earlier in the book I related how as a child I experienced the whole "mean girl" situation, which taught me how to be tough and not let people push me around. Those were difficult experiences to live through, but I was able to go back and look at that time in my life from the new perspective I now hold where I don't permit myself to be a victim. Can you now see that there are benefits to every situation? If you are unable to find the benefits—as I was in the above example—then you will continue to store memories of those difficult times as emotional baggage. That emotional baggage impacts you on an unconscious level, often expressing itself as the fear of doing something or not doing something (as I talked about earlier).

That's why it's important to constantly scan your life and love every part of it, because any part you can't love will maintain a draining, negative hold on you. Appreciate and cherish everything that you have lived through, because your experiences all form part of your unique, fingerprint-specific formula for being fabulous. I know the stories I tell people sometimes makes their head spin, but I do it because I've been a mess in my own life and was still able to turn things around. My message is that you can do, be, and have whatever you want. Just pull the plug on that mental movie that you are playing in your mind that show you failing, and start up a new movie where you see yourself living exactly the way you desire. Changing your mental state is critical for living fearlessly and going to the next level. No one said this would be easy, so you might as well play full-out.

*"The secret to your success is starts in your mind first."*

It's important that you don't let the past hold you back from living a fulfilling life. Transformation happens when the student is ready and willing to do whatever it takes to make progress. Are you ready? Or are you still giving yourself excuses, living in fear, and leaving your desires and dreams on the table?

**The Power of Your Words**

So far we've talked about the power of perceptions and they shape your beliefs. Your perceptions are like a living, breathing thing that has power over you and your life. The great thing is knowing how to change your perceptions so that they will give you the power to create an inspiring life. The same things are true about what you are *telling* yourself. You may have heard the saying, "What you think about you bring about." Do you know that experts estimate that the mind thinks between 60,000–80,000 thoughts a day? That's an average of 2500–3,300 thoughts per hour. That's incredible! So my question to you is, "Are you filling up your mind with thoughts that are empowering or destructive?"

From now on, here's what I want you to do when you are thinking about what you want to achieve. Every time you hear yourself say, "I can't do this . . . it won't happen!"—just start paying attention to the thoughts going through your head. Don't pass judgment and make yourself out to be wrong, because you know from what you've read already that negative thoughts can actually be helpful. I will never tell you to *only* think positive thoughts because that's complete crap. We are human beings and we all have negative thoughts. I am not a proponent of the "just think positive" movement, either. Most people who promote line of thinking are, ironically, among the most negative and depressed among us because they are not embracing both sides of themselves.

Dr. Norman Vincent Peale wrote his famous book *The Power of Positive Thinking* because he was feeling extremely negative about his own life. I think it's kind of funny in a way because we like to think everything is roses and sunshine on the outside. However, the fact is that no one on this planet is living a life where they are 100 percent positive 100 percent of the time. I will call out anyone who claims to always be positive, because I know that if you were to follow them around privately, you would soon enough find their other not-so-positive side on display.

This knowledge is pretty liberating, isn't it? Perhaps you're thinking, *You mean to tell me I can have a negative thought or bad day and not beat myself up for dropping the Ms. Pollyanna Perfect act?* Yes, it's true—so the next time you are having a bad day, it's okay to feel "off" and to think negative thoughts. But here's where I also want you to take it a step further, so you don't drown in a sea of negativity. First, simply be *aware* that these negative thoughts are happening to you, and give yourself permission to feel sad or pissed off, or to cry and vent to your best friend. However, after you've released the negative thoughts and feeling, you need to get shift your mental state and get back to being your empowered self. What I usually tell my clients is to just observe their thoughts, journal what they are feeling, and then go back to asking questions about the benefits they are receiving. For example, "How is feeling negative around ______ helping me to get to my goal of x?"

A few months ago I was helping a client shift her thinking around a huge contract she had lost. I ask her to start listing the benefits of losing the sale until she exhausted all possibilities. She emailed me back to say the benefits of losing the contract were that it taught her that she needed to be more present, that she needed to ask better questions, and that she needed to create more rapport with her customers. She was able to shift her gloomy mental state into a benefits-driven one. This gave her some long-term business advantages, but in the short term it allowed her to release her pent-up stress and get a good night's sleep. I told her to set up another meeting with that client for the following week to do what I call "Save the Sale." Guess what? She did and she nailed it!

Imagine how you could transform your negative thinking by simply seeing the benefits to any given situation. Seeing the benefits will always balance your mind. I've done this many times for myself in both the personal and professional areas of life. I view that occasional client that I don't get as a benefit because they would have been a pain in the a$$ to work with, and it leaves me room to attract someone who is more aligned with me and is not a drama queen. I am laughing as I write this, but it's true. I can't stand those drama clients, but every once in awhile, if I'm not on my game, they manage to slip through the cracks. When this happens I have to rebalance my mind by asking myself, *How is working with this drama client a benefit to me?* I can always find the benefits, and by doing so I'm sometimes even able to transform these people into clients I love.

Can you see that you have the power to shift your thinking in any given moment? What about those in-laws who drive you crazy, who make you want to climb the walls, head for the hills, and just disappear. Let's flip the switch and ask, *What's the benefit?* I can hear you say, "But Heather, there are no benefits. They are mean people!" This is where I challenge you to grow, because if you're forced to be in a room and spend the weekend with them, do you really want to exist under such negativity? You'd better change your attitude, because it will drive you crazy. See it as a test on dealing with difficult people. Tests like these can really sharpen your communication skills, which, incidentally, is a good thing if you're in business, where you often have to deal with challenging people (people who are more often than not your own clients and customers). I understand that you are screaming inside, thinking, *Why can't they think like me?* At this point in the book, you know it's because they have different values, and you also know you can't change people. But what you can change is your perception, so you might as well play the game.

When I am stuck in a situation where I want to bail, I practice what I preach and put this philosophy into play. Every once in awhile, for example, I receive hate mail. Yes, people will actually email me just to tell me how bad I am. I find it odd when that happens, but also curious from a human behavior standpoint. What is going on in that person's life that they have to be projecting their crap onto me? I normally delete these emails when I see them, but sometimes I scan one for a split second, which usually results in a laugh.

Recently, someone was trying to be removed from my email list. For some reason, this person was having issues unsubscribing from my email service, which has a system that spits out an automated response. Well, apparently the response it spit out didn't go over well with this person, so they emailed me in all caps TELLING ME WHAT A BAD PERSON I WAS AND HOW DARE I SEND THAT MESSAGE TO THEM. I realize, of course, that anyone who emails me in all caps doesn't understand internet etiquette, so that didn't bother me. But I found the fact that they took time out of their day to email me this message to be fascinating. I emailed them back, writing, "I see that this has caused you a lot of stress, and it's not our intention to do that. Please note you are taken out of our system." To their credit, this person then wrote back to me in a calm manner, as I has successfully been able to shift their energy. I was coming from a place of compassion; trust me, I wanted to go off on them, but why get *myself* riled up like that? I wasn't obligated to write this person back, but I decided that day to practice curiosity in understanding human behavior. I bet if I were to learn more about this person, I'd discover her life was probably a mess. Venting so much anger over a simple misunderstanding is wasted energy, and truly self-destructive. Imagine how her life could change for the better if that energy had been channeled into pursuing her passion and living her life to the fullest.

### Reprogramming Your Mindset by Becoming Aware

As you probably suspect, the reason I am sharing this story is that I want to prod you to think about where you might be wasting your mental energy with negative thoughts? It's time to focus on what matters the most to you, and where you want to go with your desires and dreams, and to do that you must practice awareness of your thoughts and words. As always, the best way to do this is to ask yourself questions:

- What are you saying to yourself?
- What are you saying to others about yourself?
- How can you change this mental state?

The following is a proven and practical formula on how to change a negative mental state:

1. Work to create a continuous awareness of your thoughts and words, specifically the negative ones that you feel are dominating your day. It requires discipline to stay on top of your thoughts, so this is something you need to practice every day.

2. Pause whatever you're doing if you catch yourself using words or phrases such as:

- I hope
- I wish
- I try
- I can't
- It will never happen
- I don't have the money
- I'm just a failure

In that moment, freeze the negative thought in your mind and replace your self-defeating language with something affirming, such as:

- I am
- I can
- I will
- I will make it happen

- I will succeed

For example, if you're looking for a new job, stay alert for thinking that says, *I can't find any jobs, all of the good ones are taken.* You won't get anywhere with that attitude. Shift your thoughts and words to, *I am in the process of aligning myself to the right paying job!* Don't stress over trying to figure out how exactly it is going to happen. Your task right now is to affirm that it *is* happening and that you're taking action in the direction of your desires.

3. Be an observer of others around you who are constantly negative with their words. Look at the areas of life they are complaining about. Can you see the correlation between what they are thinking and saying with what they are having or not having? Can you see how their self-defeating words work to prevent them from escaping their unfulfilling pattern of unhappiness and failure? I enjoy observing people at dinner parties, meetings, or really any social event. Sometimes I won't say much; I'll just study the people around me because I want to know why they think the way they do, and why they chose the words they did. This can also be used to your advantage, because if you pay attention, you will learn how successful people use words that are empowering, whereas disempowered people will use words that put themselves down. Look at their respective patterns of speech and you will see it clearly. Both sets of people are living out their internal formulas.

What words or phrases do you want to input into the operating system of your mind? Make a list of those words and practice saying them out loud. This will help you to internalize them with feeling. When you do this type of constant repetition, the words become part of you on a cellular level. You start believing what you tell yourself, and what you start believing you start *seeing* in your reality.

You can use the following list as a guide:

- I would love to . . .
- I'm inspired to do . . .
- I will do whatever it takes to . . .

*"Words are the fuel that drive you to the destination of your desires."*

Before I met my amazing boyfriend Ed, I was absolutely sick of dating men who would turn out to be both a distraction and a disaster for me. I knew that somewhere inside me I was holding onto certain beliefs that were working against my desire to find a man who would love me for me, and that if I didn't address those beliefs I wouldn't be able to break free from my pattern of unfulfilling relationships. I started paying close attention to the words I was saying to myself. This practice helped me realize that everything I believed about men was due to my perceptions. My conscious mind already knew this, but that knowledge didn't help until I reprogrammed my unconscious mind through repetition, making my new words a part of me.

Here's how I did this: I would look in the mirror, sometimes even when I was driving, and say aloud: "Any man would be so lucky to have me in their life. I am valuable and I only attract high quality men." That man mantra stuck because it tricked my unconscious mind into believing that what I wanted was possible. Within a few short weeks of reprogramming my beliefs by chanting my man mantra, Ed appeared out of the blue. And he lived just ten minutes away from me, too. The Universe has a knack of delivering with divine timing exactly what you believe in, so pay close attention to what you are telling yourself. Out with the bad, in with the good.

I hope you are now seeing how paying attention to the things you tell yourself is a key part of your La Dolce Vita Formula for living a fabulous life. Sometimes we forget how powerful we really are. That is why I want you to look at your life and know that if you've attracted some so-called bad things, you have the power to transform them into things that you desire. It's all a part of your journey and you might as well play full-out and have fun on the way. Realize that in the game of life, you're going to experience both the good and the bad. After all, this makes the journey more interesting, right? Never a dull moment!

### The Power of Using Your Body

Another powerful tool for changing your mental state is using your body. Sometimes the best way to break out of a negative mental state is to get some exercise. Get in a good workout. I love lifting heavy weights to interrupt a negative state that is causing me to feel blocked. If weights are not your thing, do some kind of movement like yoga or Pilates. Or go for a walk. We humans are built to move and be active.

When you work out you release endorphins, which are the natural feel-good chemicals that your body generates, in this case when you are exercising. Endorphins interact with the opiate receptors in the brain to reduce your perception of pain; in this way they act similarly to drugs such as morphine and codeine. In stark contrast to opiate drugs, however, activation of the opiate receptors by the body's endorphins *does not* lead to addiction or dependence. This is good for you to know because you want to develop a list of healthy, natural, viable alternatives to drugs and medication to give you a boost when you feel like you're stuck in your head. Another big benefit of exercise is that it will build positive habits in your brain, especially when done with regularity. I've also found that working out not only flushes out a bad mood, but that I often find solutions to my problems while exercising.

So exercising is one of the things I do to let loose and reset. But there are other options. If you're finding yourself too blocked and can't get your body to move intensely enough to exercise, then just the act of switching up your physical space can change your mental state. For example, let's say you are stressed about your relationship. There you are, standing in your kitchen, just waiting to crack open the tub of ice cream that's calling you for a quick sugar fix. What you can do instead is walk out of the kitchen and go somewhere else. This act alone might be enough to help you, but if not, why not leave your house and go to a coffee shop? Have some tea or coffee or anything that is going to soothe your soul. When I do this myself, I will take a book or journal and start writing, which always helps me release stress.

A simple change of scenery works wonders for me and my clients, because we're creating a new, different, healthier pattern in our brains for how to cope with stress. The more you can create these new neural pathways, the easier it is to say "No!" to self-defeating behaviors (like eating a tub of ice cream) and seek better alternatives. Eventually, your new habits for dealing with stress and negative emotions will become "baked" into you, and you'll find that you do them automatically. You'll be on cruise control then, because your unconscious mind will be synced up with your conscious mind, and in alignment with the values you want to live by. You're not coming anymore from that difficult place of forcing yourself to do what's best for you; now you act in your own best interests without having to struggle.

Let's also take a look at how you can use your body as a catalyst for creating what you want. Going back the story I shared earlier about Lynda Hamilton and the movie *The Terminator*, I used my body to get into the state of how I wanted to look. I started moving my body and walking confidently, as if I was Lynda Hamilton. (In fact, you might want to consider taking an acting class to experience what it's like to be in the mental state of a specific character and to act as if you already "have it.") As I mentioned earlier, your unconscious mind doesn't know what is real and what is not, so why not start to act like you have already achieved what you want? To do this, ask yourself questions, such as: "How does a person that has achieved x walk? How do they carry themselves?" Do a bit of research. Observe their body language, because it will reveal to you the formula of how you need to act as well.

This is not about "fake it until you make it." Rather, it's what I call "wearing the energy" of the authentic you who has already achieved what she wants. I remember doing a silly little exercise to prove this concept to myself, and it worked. I was wearing these over-the-top sunglasses that made me feel like a celebrity, so I was walking around, acting like I was a star, and just having fun. That same day, a woman stopped me and asked,"Are you someone famous?" I played around and said, "Yes, I am." I am always having fun with people and goofing around because I refuse to be one of those bored, stiff women who just has to always play by the rules.

Another incident occurred when I was a professional fitness trainer. I got the privilege to work with an officer who was on the LAPD Bomb Squad. I received a hat and shirt with the words "LAPD Bomb Squad." When I went into the grocery store wearing my gear, I noticed that people looked at me differently. I even had the checkout person ask if I was on the bomb squad. I had to laugh and break my state and tell them no, because I just couldn't keep that one in. I had fun playing that role and others, and so should you. Why is it that we are so damn serious about everything? Be more playful and lighten up your life. I want you to get out there and have fun in the practice of using your body. Model what you see other successful people are doing and watch your life transform. Everything you are doing right now, all of the techniques I am teaching you like this one, work together to get you to your goals. It's the process of adding more of the good things and subtracting some of the bad ones that will get you to your La Dolce Vita life.

### Using Creative Visualization

I want to discuss one last technique for changing your mental state, which is to visualize yourself being successful. Visualization has been my secret to creating my ideal body, attracting my amazing relationship, and building my business globally.

Years ago I was lying on the couch of an office I shared with another doctor when I was pursuing my passion as a fitness professional. During that time in my life, I really wanted to practice the art of creative visualization to prove that I could do anything that I put my mind to. I closed my eyes and started seeing an image of a person I knew. I had fun imagining specific things this person would say or do. I must have laid there for three solid hours, mentally rehearsing a specific scene. I would go back and hit the replay button and add something new each time. The very next day I felt like I was living in the movie *Groundhog Day* (which, by the way, is hilarious). The person in my mental movie that I scripted said exactly what I had imagined, verbatim. It was surreal. How is this possible? Crazy magic? Or is it that we have the power to create a mental picture and birth it into our reality?

Don't take my word for it. Do it yourself. Dedicate time and effort into doing this and see what follows. You might ask, "What about meditation?" Yes, it's similar. Meditation is about quieting your mind and observing your thoughts. When you are doing this type of training your brain waves slow down and create a more peaceful environment. Some of the most powerful leaders I know use meditation as part of their daily mindfulness routine. Mindfulness has been scientifically proven to change the brain's neuroplasticity. You can take a brain scan of someone who is stressed and isn't doing any kind of meditation practice and compare it with someone who is using this technology. The difference is night and day.

Personally, I use a hybrid of meditation and creative visualization. It works the best for me, but you need to play around with what works best for you. Just don't skip this step, because it plays an important role in helping you meet your goals. As I've mentioned several times before, your thoughts, feelings, and perceptions all impact your physiology, and knowing this is an important part of helping you live your life in the flow instead of forcing yourself to do things.

"If you get the mind right and the body will follow."

### Chapter Summary

Chapter 4 delved deeply into the all-important topic of understanding and changing your mental state. You may have all the elements of your La Dolce Vita Formula worked out, but if you can't win the mental game inside your brain you're likely to make slow progress at best.

Programming your all-powerful unconscious mind is the secret for creating the results you want. Success starts in your head, so always seek to be aware of the beliefs that are holding you back. Once you're aware of those beliefs, you have a variety of techniques at your disposal—visualization, your words, changing your mental state by moving your body—by which you can transform your self-image. When you master the mental game, you accelerate progress toward your goals and create new ways of thinking that support your quest for a fabulous life.

# CHAPTER FIVE
# CREATING CONFIDENCE AND CERTAINTY

*"Great people do things before they are ready." —Amy Poehler*

By now I want you see yourself as the master creator of your destiny, aware of your desires and values, connecting all the dots so that your mind and body are in sync, and armed with mental techniques to help you break through the illusions of your fears. Those illusions only hold power over you if you let them. It's time to put to use the tools for transformation you've been reading about so you can live the fabulous life you deserve. The next piece in the La Dolce Vita Formula ties into everything that I've been building on so far in the book: learning to create confidence and certainty about what you desire. Having the confidence to pursue your biggest desires and dreams is important because without it you will second-guess yourself. If you know how to master your confidence level you will be able to do anything. It's power is truly amazing. Ask yourself, what if you *knew* that you couldn't fail? What if you were absolutely certain that you would ultimately achieve whatever you wanted? Wouldn't you then dedicate yourself to pursuing the things that are most meaningful to you?

Having confidence is saying YES to yourself, even when you don't know all the steps. Having confidence is also about loving who you are right in the moment, and not beating yourself up for things you have done or not done. You can create unstoppable confidence by learning how to own your unique formula. You don't have to be anyone else but you.

In this chapter I'm going to share with you the secret of how to love all parts of you, past and present. You'll also learn the importance of not comparing yourself to others, because comparing yourself to others can sabotage your efforts to achieve your goals. Lastly, we will explore how to harness the power of certainty. Having certainty is the catalyst that allows you to keep taking action, even when you don't know exactly how things will work out. The combination of concepts in this chapter will power the formula to change your paradigm so you can live the most authentic version of yourself.

## Loving Yourself Where You Are Now

I used to beat myself up for not being where I think I should have been at various points in my life. I felt I wasn't good enough when I failed to achieve my financial goals, or when I kept attracting crappy relationships that left me feeling a deep void inside. And for many years I hated my body and judged myself for not being model-thin with stick legs. That didn't change until the day I stepped on the scale and realized that the numbers staring back at me were really just a starting point for me to change for the better. As I mentioned earlier, I hate scales because they don't measure your true level of progress. If they did, I would be considered obese right now, according to the archaic medical model some health professionals still use. I am laughing at this because I am a size 4, and my weight still fluctuates even now due to water, my monthly cycle, you name it. I don't care what the scale says, because I am a real woman, I have muscle, and I have the athletic body I want.

It took me awhile to get to that place of not caring about the scale; but more importantly I now love my body for how it looks. I will never be a stick-like model weighing 115 pounds and I am okay with that. I've been able to achieve a lean physique through weight training and eating a balanced diet, and in fact I eat more food than ever today because I've educated myself about food and nutrition. I now know that muscle is different than fat, and in order to get leaner you actually have to eat more calories, which is counterintuitive for most women I've worked with on the fitness level. Once I changed the way I saw myself and just started to love and appreciate my athletic shape, my body started to getting leaner as a result.

Years ago I remember looking in the mirror and hating what I saw, and the more I didn't love that current body the harder it was for me to lose weight . . . until I did exactly what I am sharing with you. I accepted where I was at, gave myself a big hug mentally, and focused on what I could do each day to improve. This strategy allowed me to make friends with the present, which I find most women can't do. They want to live in the future, but the secret to living a fulfilling life is to live in the moment. I want you to think about what you really want. Maybe, it's getting into better shape, being in an amazing relationship, having more money, or finding your life's purpose. Whatever it is, you must stop beating yourself up for not being exactly where you want to be. Trust me, I've learned this lesson the hard way and it's taken me years to understand the formula that works for me.

When I got into body building, that was my whole life. I would eat, sleep, and train, and that worked for me. Now that I run a business, staying healthy is still an important part of my formula to stay successful, and everyone around me knows that. I've created clear personal boundaries around my workouts which people respect, so it's never an issue.

Where in your life are you allowing other people to dictate what you can or can't do? I don't care if you have a partner or family, you have to put yourself first and love yourself no matter what. If you don't, the drawback is that you will project your resentment and anger onto those you love. I have see this many times with my clients and people I observe. They didn't invest enough in themselves, so they don't know who they are, and because of that they are either in horrible relationships or having their family dictate their entire life. That's no way to live, and it doesn't have to be that way. Later on, we will go over letting go of energy-draining people who you constantly feel obligated to please. You'll learn about flowing your life around these people so that they no longer slow you down. This is critical for your success, because if you keep giving your power away to others you will have nothing left for yourself.

*"If you keep giving your power away to others, you will have nothing left for yourself."*

Whenever you feel you've been thrown off track, getting back to loving yourself for where you are in this exact moment is as simple as being present. I want you to understand that every minute of each day builds in its own small way toward the bigger picture of reaching your goals. Let's go back to the topic of weight loss, or what I like to call the "creating your ideal body" goal. Let's say right now you are criticizing yourself because you're not where you want to be, even though you truly do want to change—a circumstance I completely understand.

Here's a step-by-step process that will break you out of your funk: First, just be in the moment, in the present, and take a few deep breaths. This will help you stabilize yourself for the exercise. Now, make a list of all the ways in which you are being impatient or unkind or self-hating toward yourself—get it all off your chest. It's like calling a girlfriend to vent. You want to release it, but at the same time you also want to get over yourself and stop retelling the story.

Next, tell me want do you want to create. How will getting to your goals help you to fulfill your highest personal values? Look at the seven areas of your life and start asking yourself the question, "How is taking action on x goal going to empower me in the other areas of life? What can I do right now to get me closer to my goal?"

Take a deep breath and be present in the moment; don't strive for perfection as your perform this exercise. Trying to be perfect will only make you feel like there's no room for error. There's wisdom in allowing yourself to feel "off" because it shows you how to navigate around challenges. Just chunk the process down into simple steps.

Create your list right now—and don't put it off. Writing things down is how you start forming new ways of thinking and being.

As I mentioned before, I don't believe in diets because they are not sustainable. I believe in creating new lifestyle habits that last. Would you sign up for losing twenty pounds in thirty days, only to gain it all back and then some, make your metabolism less efficient, and go back to beating yourself up again? Or would you rather lose the weight slowly, keep it off, and build your metabolism so you can even eat more, including carbs? I've managed to train my body to thrive on 200 grams of carbs a day—and sometimes more on my heavier training days—and not gain weight. I stopped demonizing carbs and changed my entire outlook and beliefs around food. I've learned to do this by repairing the metabolic damage caused my earlier lifestyle of prolonged restricted dieting and steady state cardio. Today, most people think I spend hours in the gym and eat like a bird. I actually eat tons of food, see it as fuel, and have built my metabolism back up. Doing that took me a full year of reverse dieting which is the process of slowly adding calories back in to my diet so I could get leaner.

I consult with my clients on all areas of life, helping them find their winning formula for feeling fabulous and achieving their ideal body, building their business, and attracting their ideal boyfriend. I call these the 3 B's of living fabulously—and if you're married and want a better relationship, you can have that too. Whose to say you can't have it all? You can, you just need to do it the right way, which is understanding how your mind and body work, and the power of loving and living in the present.

I know you wanted it yesterday, right? Me too, but anything worth having is work. Don't buy into get-rich-quick schemes, fad diets, or Mr. Right telling you he wants to marry you on the very first date. These are all signs that you need to run for the hills. As you know, I believe setting and creating goals that are aligned with your personal values and formula is key, because those are the goals you will accomplish. Then you will be propelled forward to set even bigger goals. If you view your goals as long-term visions, you can't help but see how chipping away at them by taking daily, inspired action you will get there in time.

And what about those times when, even if you're making progress, you despair about still not being where you want to be, of still having a long road ahead of you? Once again, the answer is to shift your mental state by asking yourself a question: "How is not getting to my goal at this moment a benefit to me?" They may not always be apparent, but there are definitely benefits to be gained as you move along on your journey. I can name one off the bat: traveling your path teaches you how to be focused and present, and to love who you are in the process of accomplishing your goal. You are learning behaviors that will be the driving force for your success. This is powerful information! Even Einstein said that time is only a illusion. What does that really mean? It means that if you keep watching the pot boil, it won't. So stop stressing out and learn how to rewire your brain for achieving long-term goals, a large part of which simply comes down to enjoying and feeling inspired by the present. After all, it's the present that you are always living in. See your path, take the steps, and repeat. It's really simple. So be aware of and resist the mental programming that diverts you from your goals by sapping your emotional and mental strength.

*"See your path, take the steps, and repeat."*

People who try to rush the process, or who hate where they are at instead of loving it, always self-sabotage, and take themselves 100 steps back from their goal. I've coached women all over the world in every area of life, so trust me, you're no different. That's why if I can help you to better understand human behavior and, most importantly, your personal formula for having confidence in yourself, then I know you'll be okay with wherever your starting point might be. You'll know it's a temporary position, because you realize that you will change the way you think and will take actions that lead you to a new level of consciousness. I love showing women just like you how to do this. As you break the old model of being critical about yourself, set goals that are aligned with who you really are, and go on to achieve them, your confidence will soar. You have just reformulated years of old programming.

### Letting Go of Comparison

I want to share an important bit of wisdom with you: Stop comparing yourself to other people! You'll increase your confidence levels and make more progress in every area of your life if you stop freaking trying to measure up against others. Easier said than done, I know, because we live in a society that preys on the weak-minded.

We see tactics in advertising that exploit envy, we see them in our Facebook feeds and elsewhere. Well, guess what? They are never going to go away. Know that the whole comparison game is based on your perceptions, and as you learned earlier in the book, your perceptions can either build you up or they can destroy you from the inside out. The good news is that you now have the tools to remake your perceptions so that they empower you.

The first question is to ask ourselves, "Why do we get into the combat zone of comparing ourselves to others?" I know for me at a very early age, I compared myself to my sister. I mentioned that she had a photographic memory and was acing tests, while I was barely passing. In fact, I can distinctly remember getting D's and some F's in the first grade and thinking what the hell is wrong with me? But why, exactly, did I think there was something wrong with me? Because I was comparing myself to my sister—and I couldn't let go of that.

As I got older, I kept developing measuring sticks for each area of life, from money to men, that were never realistic or grounded in who I really was. The result is I would put myself down each chance I got. Once I started to own my power and find my La Dolce Vita Formula, I came to appreciate my uniqueness, and the urge to compare myself to others started to fade away. The more I loved myself for who I was and didn't try to be anyone else, the more I attracted into my life money, a better relationship, and a body that I loved. Why does this happen to almost every woman who feels a void in their life? It's simple: you're comparing yourself not so much to another person, but to someone else's *values*, and therefore you're not following your unique values-based path. In truth, you are just as fabulous as the other person, just in a different way.

**Style and Confidence**

If there's one thing I learned while living in Italy, it's that Italian women who love fashion are not afraid to show their confidence through their personal style. A key part of my daily Italian coffee ritual involved people-watching, and I would always keep a sharp eye out for the latest Italian fashions. I studied each woman and I noticed that the ones who were dressed impeccably always projected a matching air of confidence.

A new client that I am working with in the fitness field is completely empowered in the areas of beauty, health, and fitness, but completely disempowered in the area of her finances. She's been at a low financial set point for years, and was always beating up on herself and comparing her life to others who were where she thought she should be. I quickly understood that her values needed to shift, since I know that a person will always take action according to their personal values (which, again, is why comparing yourself to others is a recipe for disaster). One of the first things I did with this client was to "monetize" her brilliance in the area of finance as being one her highest values. As I continue to show her how to embrace her unique formula, her confidence in the area of money will go up and she can live to her highest potential.

Sometimes I like to imagine I have magical powers when working with clients, but honestly the only thing I am showing them is their own unique formula, and how to use it to create and build a good life. It's important that you give yourself permission to shine in the way you feel is the most divine. Don't let anyone tell you it has to be done this way or that way. Break the mold, shift the paradigm, and live from your truth.

If you find yourself getting caught up in comparing yourself to someone else, try this simple mental shift, which you can do right in the moment. First, figure out specifically where you are comparing yourself with that person (or perhaps even with society as a whole). Then ask yourself, "What are their personal values demonstrating? What are they taking action on? What personal values am I demonstrating through my actions?" For example, perhaps money is the area where you are comparing yourself to another. Ask yourself, "Where do I have wealth in my life to the *same* degree?" Trust me, you do have it, it's just in a different form, a form you are valuing the most. Or maybe you feel inadequate and think you are not smart enough when it comes to talking about politics. Think again, because you're a genius in another area of life, and you need to own that. Maybe you have a brilliant mind when it comes to understanding nutrition, and in that area can run circles around the person you are comparing yourself to. Once you connect this realization with your conscious mind, you can see that you are equal to this other person. You have just empowered yourself. It might seem challenging at first, but keep asking the questions until you see it.

When you love and appreciate yourself for your finger-print-specific personal values, for the formula that makes you fabulous, you'll be immune to the attempts of others to inject their values into you. You'll possess your own strong sense of who you are and where you're headed. Your confidence levels will be at an all-time high. If you find yourself getting stuck, just return to this exercise. Each time I found myself playing the comparing game, I would use this formula to get myself back into balance. Can you see how your perceptions create everything in your life and how you can get unbalanced when you're not seeing yourself as a confident, powerful woman? There will always be someone who appears to be smarter, richer, thinner, or has a better relationship, but I encourage you to see yourself as their equal. Don't get infatuated with what you perceive others to have that you lack. Live in your Universe, which is always nudging you to be the best version of you.

**Creating Certainty**

In sales there's a phrase that goes like this: "The one that has the most certainty wins." Meaning, if you're the sales person and you have certainty about getting your client or customer results, the transaction is inevitable. There are many times and areas in your life when you experience certainty or uncertainty. You'll never have 100 percent certainty on everything, either, as there are always going to be unknown variables. But I believe that you can create more certainty in your life by living in congruence with your personal values, even when you don't know the exact steps to take and even when things don't go exactly as planned. I've faced uncertainty more times than I can count, and what I know for sure is that you can always be certain in knowing who you are at a core level, regardless of your surrounding circumstances. Use that knowledge as your GPS to guide you through the dark places.

I was living in Charleston, SC, many years ago, not knowing how I would financially survive. I was being pulled in two different directions: one was the safe route of holding down a job I loathed but that provided steady money, and the other path, filled with uncertainty, was of pursuing my passion for fitness. I remember walking to my restaurant job, hating every minute of it, working to convince myself that it was time to pull the plug and just trust the Universe in the direction I wanted to go. My confidence inspiring mantra was, "I don't know how this is going to work out, I just know it will." The truth was, I *didn't* know how it was going to work out, but my willingness to push through and grab on to a sliver of confidence was the secret to creating what I wanted at that time. I hated that job so much it was making me physically sick and robbing my soul.

**Fearless and Fabulous Female Profile**

**Marie Montessori** (1870–1952) created the Montessori philosophy of education. She was a scientist, doctor, educator, and women's right advocate. Marie had the confidence to go after her dreams, even after being denied entry into medical school because she was a woman. She persisted, and finally was accepted because of Pope Leo XIII's recommendation. Marie broke barriers, birthed a movement, and was an innovator with her ideas. She was able to pursue her passion through turbulent times, with her unwavering certainty providing the fire to keep her going. Famous people educated at Montessori Schools include Jeff Bezos (CEO of Amazon), Larry Page and Sergey Brin (cofounders of Google), Julia Child, and Anne Frank.

I love studying, learning, and reading about inspiring female figures who have paved the way. Always confident in pursuing her dreams, Marie learned how to create certainty in uncertain times. When you're feeling uncertain, take a page from history and visualize yourself being able to break through your own limitations. You can then turn your uncertainty upside down.

One night after work I was having a drink with a coworker. I told her how much I hated working at the restaurant, and how I wanted to start my fitness and coaching business. As we sat at the bar, I took the napkin from under my beer and grabbed a pen from my purse. I laughed and told her I was going to do what Benjamin Franklin did! She looked at me in confusion as I took the napkin and drew a line down the center. On the left side I wrote the word "Pro" and on the right side "Con." This was my decision-making tool for staying or leaving. I told her that I actually read that this was how Franklin would make decisions, so if it was good for Ben, it was good for Heather. I went from left to right, putting down each Pro for staying and each Con for leaving. When I tallied the results, the Cons outweighed the Pros. In that moment I had a confidence connection: "I will make more money in less time by training clients!" It was an electric feeling. In that moment I was 100 percent confident about my decision. And I didn't start telling myself a "What if this doesn't work" story, like I would always do before.

This revelation happened on a Friday. I get a call from the restaurant the next morning from one of the accountants, saying the restaurant was having an emergency meeting on Sunday. Since I was confident in knowing I was going to quit to go live my dream, I told her I was coming in anyway because I was planning to give my notice. In a low voice, she said, “Well, the reason I was asking people to come in is that the restaurant is closing.” I was shocked at this news. Then I hung up the phone and laughed because it didn’t matter to me, I had already made my decision and was free and clear. For me, the closing of the restaurant was the Universe’s way of showing me how I had all the power the entire time. We can sometimes doubt how amazing we really are, and when we do it eats away our confidence. I want you to challenge yourself to create certainty with what you want to accomplish. Do this by following your La Dolce Vita Formula. This has proven to help my clients and myself, and it will help you.

*“Ask for what you want and be prepared to get it.” —Maya Angelou*

## Chapter Summary

This chapter gave you tips and techniques to help you learn how to create unstoppable confidence, now that you’re on your La Dolce Vita journey and moving toward creating your dream life. No longer do you care about comparing yourself to others, or have time to spend criticizing your past. Filled with certainty about who you are and where you’re going, you’re on fire, ready to get to the next level.

# Chapter Six
# Aligning Your Actions with Your Desires

*"Be the energy you want to attract."—Anonymous*

## The Difference Between Inspiration and Motivation

Now that you possess the tools to work on building your confidence and certainty, we can move on to aligning your actions with your desires. When your mind and body are in alignment with what you want to create in your life, your actions will be in sync with your values. That's why I don't believe in motivation, which I view as a method of trying to *force* yourself to do something. A lot of people get confused about motivation versus inspiration, so I want to take a moment to explain the difference between the two, and tell you what you really need to know in order to achieve your goals.

When I hear someone talk about wanting to be motivated, my danger detector turns on. Why? Because the word motivation refers to using outside, extrinsic forces that compel someone to action. I know this because when I had a personal training business I would seek to "motivate" people. In the gym, I would say, "Come on—you can do it! One more rep." The problem with that approach is that it can result in someone who only comes to the gym to work out because of the influence of another person (their coach). Because they are not internally inspired, they may well go home after the workout and resume their self-sabotaging health behaviors and habits. This means the benefits of working out are temporary, and not integrated into their overall approach to life.

Let's look at the word inspiration. *Inspire* means "to come from within." When you are inspired, your brain is already in sync to take action. That's what makes inspiration so powerful; your mind and body are already working in concert to achieve your goals. You don't need external motivation, there's no one telling you do it—you automatically just take action. Imagine waking up each day, ready to get busy doing the things that you need to do to achieve your goals. Imagine being powerfully, internally inspired, always in the flow, always ready move forward.

Can you see why the motivational seminar you perhaps went to over the weekend can't provide anything near that level of positive reinforcement? Sure, the seminar might provide some benefits that maybe last a few days, but then you go back to your normal way of being because that external motivation wears off. I mean this quite literally, as you lose the endorphins that stimulated your body when you were at the seminar and were caught up in the moment, feeling you can do anything, revved up by someone up on the stage, with music playing and everyone dancing. It's understandable that in that moment you might feel as if you have super powers. But the effect is quite temporary. This is why I will never do an event or work with a client looking to get them pumped up into a temporary dopamine state. I would rather show them the science and psychology behind why they do what they do, and teach them how to get what they want through pure inspiration, which requires no motivation. It's only when you operate by your own unique formula and live by your three highest values that you can reach your true potential in any area of your life. Most people don't really know who they are, and as a result their "operating system" is hobbled by incomplete information. Think of your brain as running a complex software program that gives you instructions on which direction to go. This software program is programmable, and you can modify it to better achieve your goals. However, if you have a virus in your program you will start breaking down and self-sabotage. Your brain is a highly functioning system that is always defaulting back to your personal value system. When you are living your life by your top three personal values, it's easier to get results. Your values are there to help you find the fastest path to getting what you want. And so it doesn't matter what you do, whether you run a business, want to achieve your ideal body, get that promotion, find your purpose, or increase your income—you must understand your formula in order to stop forcing yourself to take the right actions and do the right things. You can also inspire others by learning their unique formulas. When you speak to your kids, partner, clients, boss, or friends, having already identified what their highest values are, you can inspire them to take action and see your point of view by relating what you say to their personal formula. I find that a lot of conflict within families and relationships stems from us pushing our values onto others, telling them they have to do or see things our way. But the secret to caring communication is to seek to understand what is inside of the other person's mind, what makes them tick, what their personal formula really is—once you know this, then it's like pushing the right button to get what you want. This is not about manipulation, either; it's about understanding who that person really is.

Realize that motivation, as I mentioned earlier, is a temporary fix. It's never going to work for long. But when you are inspired, what happens in the brain is you create the neural pathways to *automatically* take action. Try it! Right now, think about something you are really inspired about in your life, something where you don't need anyone to spur you to take action. You're eagerly doing it on your own, and you're waking up wanting to work out, or follow up on those prospective clients, or learn a new skill, or start putting yourself out there to date again.

**Fearless and Fabulous Female Profile**

**Miuccia Prada** (born 1948) is the CEO and one of the main stylists of the family brand Prada. Moreover, she founded the fashion line MiuMiu, named after her. She was the first stylist who worked with architects in order to create shops with a unique design, such as the ones in New York, LA, and Tokyo. Miuccia is a figure who has rewritten the rules for the world of fashion. And she's wealthy, to boot: Forbes ranks her as the third richest woman in Italy.

*"I want female dresses that can be used for work, too. I don't want women dressed like men."—Miuccia Prada*

Miuccia had a unique personal vision for the world of women's fashion. She realized this vision and is still inspiring people today. How can you work toward a future where you do something innovative that is also a unique expression of you? Don't see yourself as beneath Miuccia, but standing right beside her. Every driven woman has the power to tap into her own unique potential.

As I mentioned above, when I was a fitness professional I would try to motivate clients during workout sessions to push their limits. Interestingly, it was those clients who were internally aligned with working out and eating right who would get results outside of their sessions. They were already inspired to improve their bodies, and didn't need the external force of my cheering them on. I was just there to assist them, making sure they were getting to their goals. On the other hand, my clients that needed constant motivation from me stayed stuck, and would give me excuses as to why they went off the rails and had a bad weekend of eating.

This is why everything up I've discussed until this point is necessary for you to avoid such pitfalls. Once you find your formula, you are inspired to take action on your desires on a daily basis. My challenge for you is to decide today what you really want. Know what your top three personal values are, and visualize how accomplishing your goals is going to empower you in those areas.

*"Inspiration is your spontaneous fire within."*

## Using Your Emotions

Emotions are powerful tools for creating the neural connections that keep you in the flow. Emotions, which can be defined as positive or negative, affect your physiology. When you react to a good or bad situation, your brain produces chemicals to wire and fire those connections. The more you experience similar situations, the easier it is to get addicted to this familiar feeling. This is why it's important to understand how your emotions are like a drug. You can become addicted to wanting to relive a particular state—even a negative one—because your brain becomes familiar with it

Earlier in the book I mentioned Dr. Joe Dispenza's book *You Are The Placebo*. In that book, Dr. Dispenza describes the mechanism by which you can change your brain's chemistry. He tells you how you can create miraculous changes in your body by thought alone. Part of his technique involves pairing an elevated and positive emotion with your thoughts to encourage change. I have been able to experience and use his technology for both myself and my clients.

In Chapter 4, I related how years ago, when I was living in LA, I had a major bladder infection where I needed medical attention, but I couldn't afford emergency treatment. I had the phone number of someone who did remote healing; I was in so much pain I was willing to try anything. I got on the phone and spoke to this person, who used to be an attorney (of all things!), and he told me to relax. The phone call lasted about ten minutes—he honestly didn't do or say much—and at the end he told me to lie down for fifteen minutes and then get up. I was desperate and did exactly as he instructed. Fifteen minutes later the pain was gone. Did he heal me or was this a placebo effect? I honestly didn't care because the pain was gone and I was so thankful that my body felt 100 percent healthy again.

If you've ever experienced excruciating pain, you know exactly what I am talking about. It's not fun. This is why today I am more keen on understanding and using the mind-body connection than shoving a bunch of pills down my throat. I think Western medicine has its place, but these days I am very cognizant of what I want to put into my body. Think about it: you don't tell your finger to heal when you cut it. Your body has an innate intelligence about itself and knows when to heal a wound. If our body can do that with our finger, then what else are we capable of doing with a bit of awareness and intention?

This is what has fascinated me the most in learning about the neuroplasticity of the brain and, particularly, how our emotions impact us on a cellular level. Yes, you will have bad days, and that's okay, but the key is to not stay stuck in that level of thinking. You need to learn how you can use the power of your emotions to fuel your desires, so that you are accelerating toward achieving your goals. You can indeed change your brain chemistry to harness your emotions in this way, not to mention mix in some fun as you move forward. If you can do this on a consistent basis, you'll find yourself living at a different level of fulfillment. The problem is that most people live their lives firing off their emotions in undisciplined or negative ways, and the resulting chaos prevents them from sitting in the driver's seat of their own brain and taking charge of their life.

Remember I told you about the time when I had lost everything and got kicked out in the middle of the night by my boyfriend? The benefit from that memorable incident is it really taught me a lot about how to own my power, and it led to my discovery of a little mind hack about how to use my emotions to achieve my money goals. Every day I got myself in alignment with my goals by listening to the song "Don't Stop Believin'" by the rock band Journey. Steve Perry was the band's singer at that time, and I would begin my work day by playing that song on YouTube. But I just didn't play it one time, I played it for hours straight as I was working. The song elicited such a strong positive emotion in me that I was taking daily, inspired action. This mind hack was one of the most powerful techniques I've ever discovered, and I came across it by accident long before reading any of the literature on understanding the mind. I hit the replay button over and over, and it was as if someone was inside of my brain, busily rewiring it to help me take action.

One day, I realized that things were really beginning to line up for me. I was so inspired by the action I was taking and my positive attitude, I couldn't believe that my bank account was reflecting what I was feeling. I was in the flow and loving it. I decided that I wanted to meet Steve Perry, the man who sang *my* song, and let him know that "Don't Stop Believin'" changed my inner and outer worlds. I thought, *I wonder where he lives?* So I Googled the phrase "Where does Steve Perry live?" and found out he resided in Del Mar, CA. My next thought was, *What are my chances of meeting him?* Never say never, right? I went on with my day and four hours later, out of the blue, I get an email that said I had won a two-nights stay at a hotel called L'auberge and—guess what?—it was located in Del Mar! Freaky, right? How can you explain that? So I went there and had an amazing time, and although I never met Steve Perry that incident showed me how powerful emotions can be when creating and achieving your desires.

*"Don't stop believin'*
*Hold on to that feelin'"*
*—Steve Perry, lead singer for Journey from 1977 to 1987*

**Creating Your La Dolce Vita Playlist**

Why not try the favorite song technique for yourself? It might do wonders! Pick what task you want accomplish and continuously replay your go-to song or video. You can even create favorite lists with services like Spotify or iTunes. I've found that this is a great way to rewire your brain. As I've been mentioning all along, 95 percent of your beliefs, habits, and actions are dictated through your unconscious mind, which you are capable of reprogramming. I know that sometimes I sound like a broken record to my readers and private clients, or when I am speaking, doing videos, or doing my show. I repeatedly share the same concepts, but in different ways, to get people to connect with my message—first on a conscious level, which then seeps into their unconscious mind, the master control switch for everything you desire. Learn now to reprogram it for success and watch your world change

## Connecting to Your Intuition

Have you ever had an inner nudge to do something, but you didn't follow through? Or maybe you did act on it. Have you ever been curious about why—or why not—you do or don't take action? Let's talk about intuition, which I describe as your unconscious mind seeping into your conscious thought processes. It's something you should listen to when it appears. You can use intuition to, for example, almost automatically tune into what your body needs when you're eating. It will help you know what foods are best for you right now. I've been able to use intuitive thinking in every area in my life, and when I don't I pay the price.

One day when I was living in New York City, working on an art project, I decided to go across the street to a small bodega to get a snack. Then, oddly, a voice inside of me said, "Don't go! Wait five minutes." I thought to myself how strange that was, but I decided to pay attention to that voice and stayed inside. A few minutes later I heard something outside go pop-pop-pop. I raced to my window and saw a man running from the bodega, firing a gun as he went. I would have been exactly in that spot if my inner voice hadn't told me to wait. Grateful I wasn't caught up in the crossfire, this incident taught me to start paying attention to everything.

**A La Dolce Vita Lesson**

Here's a great experiment you can conduct to learn how to listen to and trust your intuition. Pay closer attention to your intuition, and write down what it tells you every time you get an inner nudge to act—or not act, as in the New York case described above—on something. Track your results over time. After a while, assess your experiment's data. Has listening to your intuition helped you achieve favorable outcomes? Has not listening to your intuition resulted in bad decisions or setbacks? Make this a lifelong practice. The more you tune in to your powerful unconscious mind, the easier it will be to take actions that align themselves with your deepest goals.

What are you ignoring in your life right now? What is your intuition trying to tell you? I want you to start paying attention to your intuition—and trust it. It is a powerful force in guiding you toward your desires. It's unfortunate that we tend to dismiss our intuition and go about our days aimlessly. If you want to create a fabulous formula for your life, then you need to work on harnessing this super power. Everyone has it, but most don't understand or use it.

*"Your intuition is your soul's compass guiding you to your own truth."*

## Creating Your La Dolce Vita Vision

The clarity of your vision for your life will determine your outcome, and any detail you leave out of that vision is a magnet that will attract chaos. If you don't believe me, look at your life right now and examine exactly what you are telling yourself about wanting to achieve a better body, attract a boyfriend, or have more money. What words, precisely, are you using to describe these desires? Are you really, truly clear in how you phrase them? Or is there cloudiness in how you describe the things you want?

When I am speaking to a group of entrepreneurs, this is part of the formula I show them. It helps them attract better clients and align themselves with what they want in their business vision. I myself, at times when I haven't been crystal clear with my own wording, have attracted crappy, entitled clients who couldn't pay me. I would get so pissed for attracting them into my business and life, until I recognized that in actuality they served to provide feedback to my conscious mind when I wasn't clear enough. This is why I want you to take the time to get clear on what your goals are. Get specific and detailed with your wording. What is it that you want to do, be, and have for the rest of your life? If you don't know this then you're living in uncertainty; you'll find yourself living your life out of desperation. I know this because I would invite chaos into every area of my life where I wasn't true to myself and clear on what I wanted.

*"When your vision is clear, you will attract the right, people, places, and resources into your life."*

The formula is like a math equation:

**DO + BE = HAVE**

The questions you want to ask yourself are:

- What do I want to do?
- What do I want to be?
- What do I want to have?

If you've worked your way through the book to this point, you should now have the answers to those questions: you know your values and your goals, and you can write down your personal equation. There are several ways you can write your equation, and we don't need to overcomplicate this. When I am working with clients who are focusing on their business vision, I have them create something similar to a personal equation. Here's an example from a client for whom I helped create a daycare center business:

**La Dolce Vita Vision Statement**

My purpose is protecting children and providing a fun, engaging, and accelerated way of learning through the XYZ Daycare and School. I have multiple locations that are located in X County that are open 24 hours a day.

I have trained the right staff to assist me in the day-to-day operation of providing excellent childcare and accelerated learning. I empower young girls and women through my story that you can speak your truth and own your power in all areas of life. I do this through speaking and mentoring. I am committed to the families I serve. I strive to give parents complete peace of mind while being seen as a shining example of what a quality childcare center should be. I encourage our children to be independent thinkers and lifelong learners.

If you don't have a business, your formula can follow a similar format and flow. What is the most important thing you want to include in your La Dolce Vita Vision Statement? Think about all seven areas of life. For example, if you have kids, make sure that in your LDV Vision Statement you write about what you want for your kids, and how you will assist them to be the best versions of themselves they can be. For instance, you could write: "I'm empowering my kids to live an inspired life and I do that by example. I will pay for their college tuition and support them in anything they want to pursue." The above sample is just a brief excerpt of what you can write; you want to go into as much detail as possible.

Another example would concern your health and fitness. In your vision statement, you could say things like, "I have the health and vitality that allows me to be active in my daily life. I have a lean and fit body, and I eat food that energizes me. I consistently work to educate myself on holistic health and mindful practices that keep me looking and feeling young." You may also incorporate going to seminars or workshops, or note books you want to read about specific areas of health. Go into into the details of how and when you are going to take action.

Take the time to write all this down, and then reflect on your words. Once your La Dolce Vita Vision Statement is complete, be sure to reread it every day, because that is part of the programming process to align your actions to your desires. Your thoughts have great power, so if you pair the repetition of daily reading with a positive emotion, you start internalizing your vision's message, and it becomes a part of your formula for living a fulfilling life. You'll find yourself taking action. You will break through the challenges, even when things get tough. I was reading an article the other day about Jeff Bezos, who is the richest man in the world as of this writing. The article describes how he made a decision to leave his cushy Wall Street job to pursue and create his personal vision. Take a page from Bezos's life and see the bigger picture of your life and vision.

Whenever you read your LDV Vision Statement, always ask yourself if you need to change any of the words or phrases. As you proceed down your path, your vision will clarify, so you'll sometimes need to fine-tune your wording. As I mentioned earlier, the clearer you are the better you will align yourself to what you desire. So keep your statement up-to-date. I do this every single day.

One time I was frustrated by having some prospective clients tell me they would "think about it" in terms of working with me. If you're in sales, you know what that means. As I was reading my vision the next morning, I said "Yes, I need to make an adjustment to my statement. I need to add the words ACTION TAKERS to describe my ideal clients!" The funny part of this story is that the same day I added those words, I had my prospective clients become action takers and say yes.

Don't put this task off. In fact, put the book down and start writing out your vision. It's one of the most critical things you can do, and is far more powerful than just saying a bunch of affirmations. As you write and revise, keep asking yourself, "Have I left any details out? Is what I'm writing aligned with who I am?" After you have completed your statement, let those words become your mission, your mantra, your *formula* for creating a fearless, fabulous, and fulfilling life.

**Italy's Vision Statement for Coffee**

I found coffee to be my spiritual home and inspiration while in Italy. Drinking anything with milk after breakfast is supposedly a no-no to Italians; they are adamant about their digestion, and consider it bad to drink milk after breakfast hours (but I broke the rules and did it anyway). Here's how you drink coffee like a true Italian:

Rule #1: You must never ask for a double shot like we do at Starbucks. All sizes are standard for each drink, so there's no upsizing.

Rule #2: Although I found myself hanging out in cafés for hours, a true Italian gets in and out. This is radically different from camping out at your local Starbucks. What I admired about Italians is that it's like they were on a mission when they went to get their coffee.

The Italians have created their own inspired vision for coffee, and from the barista to the customer, everyone is clear about what their role is. This insight about Italian coffee culture has allowed me to create clarity for my business and life. My mantra is "All good things happen at Starbucks," or any coffee place for that matter. The secret is to find your *dolce* (sweet) place where you can sit down and happily work on fulfilling your life's vision.

After you've created the first draft of your La Dolce Vita Vision Statement, it's time to sync up your brain and take things to the next level of alignment by visualizing yourself exactly as you want to become. I call this the Immersion Vision Technique, what means you immerse yourself into becoming exactly what you've written down in your vision. I've been using visualization for years, and it's a truly powerful method for changing your unconscious mind. There are many ways you can go about this, but what I've found to work remarkably well, since we live in the digital age, is to use videos to assist with this practice. Every day after you read your LDV Vision Statement, hop over to YouTube, set your timer on your phone, and listen for a while to inspiring videos that are aligned with your goals.

For example, if you're wanting to create a better or healthier body, try watching videos about people who have successfully transformed their health. Seek to understand what they did to accomplish this. Watch one video multiple times or multiple videos one time each at a given sitting; whatever works for you. Then visualize yourself doing what those people did. Get detailed, and imagine yourself taking the specific actions that lead to the results you want. So forget about binge-watching your favorite Netflix show and instead focus on using this technique to create the life you really want. If you can fit in doing this twice a day, then that's even better. The results for my private clients have been amazing, too, by helping them imprint a new and compelling self-image into their unconscious mind.

I am so passionate about using this technique because it's a simple method that works. Also, if you have issues calming your mind through meditation, I've found visualization to be a brain hack that really works to settle you down. Make visualization a mental habit; you'll quickly start changing your beliefs. Soon after changing your beliefs, you start to see undeniable results on the outer level as you take self-aligned action in your life.

### Chapter Summary

Internal inspiration—different from external motivation—is the ultimate force to power you toward achieving your deepest desires. In this chapter, you wrote with crystal clarity your own personal La Dolce Vita Vision Statement. When you pair the inspiring words from your Vision Statement with taking actions that are aligned with your values, each morning you'll wake up ready to jump out of bed to get your day started! Don't leave any detail left out of your Vision Statement, as it will invite chaos and confusion into your life. The clarity of your life will determine exactly what you receive.

# Chapter Seven
# Letting Go and Getting into the Flow

*"What's the greater risk? Letting go of what people think—or letting go of how I feel, what I believe, and who I am?" —Brene Brown*

The information in this chapter will be most useful if you are now following your life formula and using the various strategies discussed earlier in the book and seeing results, even if they are small. If you're not seeing results, take a step back and thoroughly review everything you're doing. It could mean you are missing a step. Again, don't be hard on yourself if this is the case. This is all a learning process. Also keep in mind that "results" can be as simple as simply feeling different. Feeling different inside is the first step to changing your outer world. Most people want to see results first before they commit to believing in something. Don't' do this, because as I've shown you, the unconscious mind is controlling everything behind the scenes, and you have to master that inner part of you to achieve your goals. I've been doing this for years, and I still fail miserably when I don't follow my formula; and I always create success when I do. You're no different, and once you fully appreciate how powerful your mind is when it comes to controlling your body and taking action, you'll never go back to your old ways of thinking and being.

This doesn't mean you'll never have challenges. Challenges are a necessary and inevitable part of life. It's how you *perceive* challenges that will make or break you. The main reason why most people fail to meet their goals is that they don't have their unique formula figured out, they don't have access to the steps and techniques mentioned in this book, and they lack a clear vision of what they really want or how they are going to get there. I want you to repeat after me: "Challenges are necessary to get what I want. I am attracting challenges that are inspiring to me." Simply understanding this concept will drive you to be successful in any goal you want.

Sadly, I too often see people quit because of challenges. When I first started coaching clients, I didn't realize how common this was. I soon realized that the ones who threw in the towel and blamed me for not getting them to their goal didn't want to take responsibility for their actions. Conversely, the clients that got amazing results were rock-solid in how they perceived challenges. They would find their way through, around, or under any obstacle that was thrown at them. As I started working with more and more clients, I inserted into my personal La Dolce Vita Vision Statement that I only wanted to work with women who could take on challenges. I was tired of being blamed for other people's unwillingness to take responsibility. It's exhausting working with people who won't let me help them, because after all, I too was once disempowered in my life. I had to endure many challenges to get to where I am today, all of which hinged on my taking responsibility for my life.

Today I work with winners. I select who I want to work with and the minute I sense someone is not committed to doing the inner and outer work necessary to improve their life, I let them know that we're not going to be a good fit. Think about it this way: anything you want to have or master in your lifetime is going to require work. You'd better realize that if you want to be the best at something, you will most certainly attract challenges. There's a misconception about challenges—they can actually be fun. When tackling a challenge, you're stretching your brain "muscles" to find solutions, and when you do your mind evolves to the next level of perception. What if you could look at challenges as being sources of inspiration? What if you took the opportunity each challenges presents to ask yourself empowering question? Wouldn't that change your experience for the better? What if you embraced each challenge with enthusiasm, knowing that you grow stronger through challenges and thereby accelerate the accomplishment of your goals? So you can see challenges as either good or bad; just realize you are right either way.

*"Il dolce far niente."*
*("The sweetness of doing nothing.")*

## Getting Unstuck and Getting Out of Your Own Way

Yes, you will get stuck on your journey to making more money in your business, finding the perfect job, creating your ideal body, and attracting Mr. Right. Achieving what you once thought was impossible won't always be easy, but that's all right. We're only human. Our bundle of traits means we are both action-takers and susceptible to being lazy. Give yourself permission to not be perfect, because you're not. No one is. As we advance in robotics, I wonder if programmers will intentionally create artificial intelligence with flaws? If they want to mimic humanity, they should. You can't be a true human if you're perfect. Furthermore, to be honest, wouldn't life would be boring without a challenge or two?

I know you might not agree with me, so let me say it another way. Imagine you were in a relationship with someone who said, "Do whatever you want," and they always agreed with you about everything. While at first glance this might seem great, I guarantee you that after a while you would get very bored. Yes, you want to avoid being in a relationship where you are constantly fighting, but a strong, balanced relationship will certainly mix in a few challenging elements.

**How to Deal with Difficult Relationships**

Sometimes a serious issue develops with your partner, where he will infect you with his fears and negative beliefs. This might cause you to stop moving forward and give up on your goals. But giving up will only attract more chaos into your life. The repercussions can be severe, including getting sick and becoming emotionally detached from your partner.

It's your job to stay true to yourself. You know that if you can follow your own La Dolce Vita Formula, you will live a fulfilling life. Please take that knowledge seriously. However, you must also be compassionate with your partner. What if your partner is adamant about telling you that you can't do what you want? My personal opinion is that you may need to reevaluate your relationship, because it's clear that there's not enough effective communication taking place, and that neither you nor your partner are getting their needs met.

Sound harsh? Yes, it is, so tread with caution. But ultimately it's your life. Why would you want anyone else telling you what you can or can't do. Don't get me wrong—I am not suggesting you do something crazy that goes radically against your partner or seeks to harm him. What I've found in working with clients and through my own experiences is that typically the partner is projecting his own fears onto you. If you understand this, you have a real chance to put in the work to improve the relationship so you both get what you want.

This is particularly true until you grow as a couple and better learn each other's formulas. If I have a disagreement with my boyfriend, we are both conscientious enough to work through it and actually refine our relationship formula. We are never stagnant, so our relationship unfolds beautifully as we learn how each of us is unique. This is why you need to get your partner on board with supporting you in your goals. If you don't, you'll face extra friction whenever you go after something.

Let's say you want to start your own business, but your partner has issues about money and frequently challenges you about it. He is often trying to get you to see his side, and might drive you to quit your dreams. I encourage you to never let go of your goals, especially if you're at a place where you're in alignment with what you want. If you go against yourself, you will resent your partner and create more tension in the relationship. Yes, I think it's important to hear your partner's viewpoint so that they feel respected. In fact, one thing you can do to try to make things better is seek to understand what exactly your partner fears about your pursuit of your goal. However, in the end your bedrock position needs to be, "I would love for you to support me on this goal, even if you don't understand it." No matter where the challenge is coming from in your life, you need to deal with it head on.

*"When I let go of what I am, I become what I might be. When I let go of what I have, I receive what I need." —Lao Tzu*

Challenges can take many forms. They can feel like roadblocks, or like street signs telling you to stop or yield. If you're serious about achieving your goals, find a way to power through. I want you to see obstacles as tests that you're willing to pass, one after another, by getting into the proactive mode of asking empowering questions. Each time you ask an empowering question, you start rewiring your thinking. Perhaps you've heard the phrase, "The quality of your questions determines the quality of your life." Believe me, it's 100 percent true, because it means you are either programming your mind for success or for failure. Most people rarely ask themselves good questions, so they program their minds for failure without ever realizing it.

### A Formula for Getting Yourself Unstuck

Whenever you find yourself stuck and can't get going again, ask yourself the following questions. They are designed to help you take action again.

- What can I do *right now* to make myself feel better?
- What action can I take to find a better path?
- Who can I talk to who might have the answer to my problem?

- Is there someone I can hire who can help me?
- Who can I talk to so I can just vent?
- Where can I go right now to quiet my mind?
- What can I listen to, read, or watch that will help me through this temporary rough patch?

Getting unstuck doesn't have to take hours, weeks, months, or years, if you know how to do it. I wish that years ago I had known about this list of questions, or similar tools. I could have saved myself time and mental energy, and found solutions to my problems much faster. But since I lacked such tools back then, I often felt like my life was being led by a sloth. When it comes to solving problems, I don't want to be in sloth mode! I'm sure you feel the same way too. It's frustrating to be smart and yet still you can't get out of your own way. Certainly no one taught you in school how to problem-solve. Instead you just got good at memorizing and regurgitating information. And you either passed or failed at this. That's why I believe most teaching in schools is outdated and ineffective. We need to find new ways to empower children that will show them how to be confident and powerful leaders who can take on everyday problems and solve them.

My boyfriend is actually a masterful teacher to his daughter. If she's faced with a problem, he will talk to her as if she's an adult and walk her through the logic of problem-solving. In my book, he deserves the father of the year award! He's trained her brain so well that she often beats us when we are playing gin rummy, and she's only 11. If you have children, you too can teach them how to work through the obstacles confronting them, which will help them build powerful problem-solving skills and strategies that will benefit them their entire lives.

### Energy Drains and People Pleasing

Do you have a hard time telling people no? Have you noticed that this behavior often gets in the way of you achieving your goals? You do yourself a huge disservice when you don't say "no" to people whose often trivial requests take you away from acting on your own behalf. Plus, if you keep this behavior pattern up, it will eventually make you sick. You will start resenting others, and that resentment will be unconsciously built up in your body. These unconsciously stored resentments will ultimately be manifested through illness, disease, and emotional outbursts. You'll be stuck in a continuous negative feedback loop until you do something about it.

Have you ever been in a relationship with someone who, one day, finally burst out emotionally over something silly, like your forgetting to put away the dishes? It's trivial, isn't it? But people explode like this because they have been suppressing their emotions. Anything you suppress will eventually get expressed in one form or another. This is why knowing and living by your unique formula is always the answer. It keeps you on track, and guides you on when to tell people no and when to say yes. Are there people in your life who don't approve of what you want to do? If so, you have to either change how you interact with them so that they become more accepting of your goals, or you have to let them go. Energy drains can come in many forms: people, locations, or even tasks that you hate doing. Don't put up with these blockages. Protect your energy! This makes more sense once you comprehend that everything *is* energy. In fact, if you were to go into a room of people and join a conversation, just by standing next to a person without saying a word you could pick up on his or her energy. I am very protective of mine. I've had to ditch toxic friends who were bringing my energy down, and break up with boyfriends who wanted to change me or who didn't believe in me. I've also had to delegate to other people certain tasks in my life that were simply too draining for me to deal with. You can't do it all, so you, too, should strongly consider delegating some things. Each and every thing that saps your energy slows your progress toward your goals.

### The Formula for Releasing Your Energy Drains

Create a list of energy drains in your life by thinking about people and tasks that are taking you further away from you goals. After you've got your list ready, create an action plan detailing what specifically you will do about each item you've listed. Don't postpone this! You need to develop a strategy for dealing with each of your life's energy drains, or they will continue to sabotage your goals. Yes, you have to make yourself *that* important. Your goals come first. No one said this would be easy, because if it was, then everyone would be exactly where they wanted to be.

It goes without saying that you need to use your discretion; you can't just dump everyone around you. But work toward making the changes you need to make in your environment so you can continue down your path. You may not need it, but I am giving you permission to live *your* life and to stop being afraid of what everyone thinks. You will always anger a few people as you reach for your goals—it's inevitable. But trying to say yes all the time and pleasing others is an exhausting recipe for building up resentment and frustration.

*"Surround yourself with high-vibe people who want to see you succeed."*

### How to Be Focused and in the Creative Flow

I've written at length about how being aligned and in the flow are the secrets to achieving any goal you want. But there's more to that equation: you also need to tap into your creative flow and be able to focus. The average person at work loses their focus about every three minutes. Whether you work for someone else or you're an entrepreneur, you know how easy it is to get distracted. Facebook is a great example of a time waster: checking in with your friends, posting your status update, watching dog or cat videos. The dirty secret is that Facebook was built from the ground up to get you to behave that way. Its algorithms are masterfully designed to give users dopamine fixes.

I've been able to train myself to use Facebook and other time stealers more strategically, but in the beginning I was sucked in by them, just like everyone else. Then I noticed that I became less efficient in my work, felt drained and unfocused, and forgot about being creative. In summary, I was left feeling flat and uninspired. I do like Facebook, but it and similar social media sites can be highly problematic in reaching your goals. The good news is that, as with so many other things, you can rewire your brain to not let this happen.

**The formula for being disciplined and focused:**

1. **First pick a good time for you to focus working on your goals.**

Whether it's morning, afternoon, or at night, choose a time that will consistently work for you. Whatever time it is, just make sure you block it out on your calendar.

2. **Record everything in your calendar**

I live by my calendar, where I have my workouts, client calls, and personal errands all set. Disciplined use of my calendar allows me to have a single focus at a time and not be all over the place, trying to multitask.

3. **Set a timer for each goal you are working on.**

As I sit here in Starbucks writing this section of the book, I have a timer set to keep my schedule on track. Smart time management allows me to get done in much shorter time frames things that used to take me hours or weeks. A major side-benefit of optimizing your time is that you train your brain to focus better. When you improve your focus you accelerate the time frame for reaching your goals.

**4. Take small breaks.**

If you are working on a creative project, it's helpful to get up and stretch. This gets the blood flowing and takes your eyes off the computer screen.

**5. Practice mindfulness.**

Anytime you can sit quietly and meditate for a few minutes, you'll improve your ability to focus and will allow your creativity to flow.

I've been able to set short, intense deadlines for every book I've written by using these exact strategies. Also, I like to find spaces and places to work that are inspiring because I find that impacts my energy. When I competed in bodybuilding and fitness competitions, I learned how great the power of focus can be because to do well I needed to eat specific foods at specific times, work out everyday, and set a deadline for when I needed my body to be ready for the event.

You probably aren't going to compete in bodybuilding and fitness, but mastering the skill of focus will help you in anything you endeavor to do. If this book is about anything, it's about how everything starts in your mind. Get your mind right and the body will follow. Discipline yourself to master the art of focus and you'll surprise yourself with what you can do. Ordinary thinking will get you ordinary results, but masterful discipline of the mind will open up any door.

**Fearless and Fabulous Female Profile**

**Isabella Rossellini** (born 1952) is an Italian actress, filmmaker, author, philanthropist, and model. Her father, Roberto Rossellini, was the titan of mid-century Italian cinema—a creator and the greatest practitioner of the classical neo-realist style. And her mother, Ingrid Bergman, is among the greatest actresses of all time. Isabella, who was born in Rome in 1952, underwent an operation for appendicitis at the age of five. At 11, she was diagnosed with scoliosis. In order to correct that condition, she had to undergo an 18-month ordeal of painful stretching exercises, body casts, and surgery on her spine, using pieces of one of her shin bones. Consequently, she has permanent incision scars on her back and shin.

To her credit, she didn't let her physical issues stop her because she went on to pursue careers in modeling and acting. Isabella was also determined from a very young age to be financially independent. This goal came from her seeing her mother left with next to nothing when Isabella's father died. This created in the young Isabella a strong value to be financially independent.

Look at where you've endured challenges in your life and how they shaped your highest personal values. Do things which you perceive as missing from your life influence who you are today?

## Chapter Summary

To exist in a state of flow and creativity, you must get yourself unstuck from people and thought/behavior patterns that are draining your energy. Let go of the fear of failure and give yourself permission to go after your biggest desires and dreams without worrying about what others might think of you. This chapter gave you a tried-and-true formula to get unstuck, so use it whenever you're blocked to get yourself flowing again. Once you're flowing, you can use this chapter's formula for being disciplined and focused to keep charging forward.

# Chapter Eight
# The Power of Gratitude

*"Appreciating what shows up in your life changes your personal vibration. Gratitude elevates your life to a higher frequency." —Oprah Winfrey*

You may have heard the phrase "Have an attitude of gratitude," but are you practicing that philosophy in your life? Do you know that gratitude is one of your most powerful internal forces, and you can use it to align or realign your goals? So with that in mind, let me ask you a question: Are you grateful for where you're at right now in your life, or are you beating yourself up for not being where you want to be? If it's the latter, stop! The imbalanced perceptions caused by the powerful emotion of ingratitude actually shrink your brain—not good! Physiologically speaking, when you're focusing on not having enough, or if you tell yourself, *I will only be happy when* . . , you're creating a recipe for making yourself sick. If you don't believe me, take a look at people you know who are constantly complaining. Do they seem healthy to you? Are their bodies on a slow, downward spiral?

When I had my fitness business, I trained this one guy who did nothing but complain about his life. I found it fascinating that he would get sick constantly, and mentally be all over the place. Back then I wasn't aware as I am today about how thoughts and emotions are either an elixir for good health or a potion for bad health. If you keep thinking things are horrible, you can expect your headaches and migraines to perpetuate. You can't have a balanced body with an imbalanced mind.

I remember living in LA and renting a small bedroom where I slept on a mattress on the floor because I didn't have enough money to buy a bed. It made for some bad nights of sleeping. Then I had the opportunity to leave that life for a better one in Charleston, SC, where I had a hot-water shower and a comfortable bed to sleep in. I thought I was rich. Each day I would perform a gratitude ritual of feeling thankful for the hot shower and my bed. I turned this practice into a lifelong habit, and it's been interesting to see over time how things started to shift in my life once I began to really appreciate the good things I had. We get so caught up in what we feel is not working, or what we don't have, that we neglect to embrace the valuable things that exist right now in our world. I don't care if it's the shirt on your back, there's always something that you can be grateful for.

### Creating Your Gratitude Formula

Creating your own Gratitude Formula is a great way to instantly snap yourself out of self-sabotaging patterns. I've designed a specific program that goes with this book to help you create your own Gratitude Formula. Let me break down it down for you:

1. Pick a daily time—usually either in the morning or at night—when you will be able to write down what you are grateful for.
2. Choose 5–10 things that you feel 100 percent grateful for. These might be the simplest of things, such as the following:

- I'm grateful for my bed because I had a great night's sleep.
- I'm grateful for my amazing health and I love my work.
- I'm grateful to my partner for being able to work through our misunderstandings.
- I'm grateful for my fabulous clients who love working with me.
- I'm grateful for my kids being able to communicate with me.

Pick out specific things in your day that happened during that day or the day before. Yes, you can also express gratitude about more general aspects of your life, but I find that the more specific you are, the more powerful the impact. Through this practice, you are essentially wiring and firing those pathways in your brain to create the highest emotion, which is love. Love is the most powerful force on the planet, and the more you can build up its presence in your mind, the stronger your immune system will be. Like I've said before, don't take my word on this—practice activating your own Gratitude Formula and watch what happens.

*"The secret to having it all is knowing that you already do."*

### The Science and Practice of Saying Thanks

Now you have your Gratitude Formula that you will practice every single day. Be consistent in expressing gratitude, because it will inspire and protect you. According to a recent article in *Business Insider*, stress changes the structure of the brain, which can affect cognitive functioning and impair memory and well-being (although, fortunately, the brain can recover). This is why if you can't be grateful for past and present events that you've perceived through your senses as bad, eventually it will impact your physiology in a negative way on a cellular level. Why is this important? Well, just as thoughts can make you well, they can also make you sick.

When I work with clients privately, I use a specific scientific method that helps people transform resentment and imbalanced perceptions into love. I was recently coaching a client who had invested a lot of money in her business, which she co-owned with other people. She complained to me that she hasn't really made any money, and I could tell that we needed to shift her attitude quickly or she would continue to follow the same path, limited by her own beliefs. I helped turn the situation around by getting her to focus on what she was grateful for. I led her through a series of questions that uncovered the benefits she was receiving from her (perceived) negative experiences.

Are there things about yourself that you do not love, or are there thing in your life that you feel guilt or shame about? Who in this moment are you resenting, allowing them to occupy precious mental real estate? The people my client invested with weighed heavily on her mind; my goal was for her to see that every situation can have a silver lining. Write it down now, and don't move on until you can see the benefits of each person and situation.

Write down people past or present who are still a trigger for you:

1. ______________________________

2. ______________________________

3. ______________________________

4. ______________________________

5. ______________________________

After you've finished your list, think hard about the benefits you receive from each of these problematic relationships. As I mentioned, there's always a silver lining. If you can "flip the script" with the difficult people in your life, you free up a tremendous cache of previously trapped mental energy.

**Italian Gratitude**

Italians are not perfect, and their country has its problems and issues, but what they lack in some areas they make up for in the way they celebrate life in the simplest, most relaxed ways. They are grateful for their personal relationships and happy to make time for others, always willing to talk and share their gratitude for each day. While I was living in Italy, on more than one occasion I noticed Italians spontaneously break out into song and dance. If you're a visitor to Italy who is willing to learn Italian and embrace the country's traditions and way of life, you'll be warmly received by the natives, who will go out of their way to welcome and help you. Above all, you need to love Italy as it is, warts and all. The exact same lesson applies to your own la dolce vita.

## The Formula for Receiving

My intention is that you fully understand how powerful your mind is in creating what you want (as well as what you don't want), not to mention it's impact on sickness and health. Having this information at your fingertips is life-changing because it frees you from fretting that there's something wrong with you. There isn't anything wrong with you, at least not anything that is outside your power to change. You know when you are getting in your own way and you know exactly what is stopping you.

You're like the scientist in your own experiment of life. If you don't like the results, then change the conditions of your experiment (your life). Once you integrate this bit of wisdom, coupled with following your own unique formula for life, you will wake up feeling inspired each and every day.

Having worked with so many women from all over the world, I can share with you that the inability to receive is a big block for achieving ones goals. Women traditionally play the role of being the nurturers, even if they're not a mother. You probably see this urge within yourself, too. You get pulled into a million different directions, and as a result you don't practice the art of receiving. I say "art" because anything you want in life has to come from having self-mastery, which, like artistic ability or anything else worth doing, takes time to develop. When you were little you were probably very open to receiving, such as when you asked for something like an ice cream cone or a pair of shoes. Conversely, growing up in a hostile environment can impair one's ability to receive. Either way, the secret to receiving lies in valuing yourself.

Back when I kept attracting crappy relationships, I was trapped by self-defeating mental patterns that I was finally able to break once I started believing that I was a woman who was valuable. Even the smartest female CEOs I know have this issue of not fully valuing themselves. This unhappy pattern doesn't discriminate with age, race, or gender, either (men, too, can experience it). Until you value yourself, don't expect anyone else to because they can sense that you are not in a place of receiving.

One of the most powerful exercises I teach about the art of receiving is to know your value, so let me summarize the system I've created that shows you how to do this. Let's say you are a single woman who is having relationship issues similar to the ones I've told you about from my life. You are an amazing woman, yet you keep falling into the same pattern of dating men who devalue you. You give so much and yet feel empty inside. Why is this? It's simple: you just don't value yourself enough. I know this to be true, because I am a smart woman and I had precisely the same issue. Again, it has nothing to do with your IQ and everything to do with your sense of self-worth. So how do you raise your value and attract a better man who will love and adore you for who you are? First, you *must* love yourself. When you love yourself you raise your value, and other people will pick up on this.

So let's get into the exercise. List the things below that you love about yourself (and don't you dare tell me it's nothing!)

1. ______________________________
2. ______________________________
3. ______________________________
4. ______________________________
5. ______________________________

After you've made your list, I want you to ask yourself where in the past you have pretzeled yourself to fulfill the needs of an unsuitable man? Where have you given up your gym time, alone time, and creative time for someone else, only to come to resent that person later?

List below where you've given up your identify and stopped living your truth. Pick the most painful moments where you have attracted chaos as a result of not following your formula:

1. ____________________________
2. ____________________________
3. ____________________________
4. ____________________________
5. ____________________________

When you get into a relationship you become infatuated. And when you're infatuated you become chemically bonded to the other person and believe you are in love, but in fact it's the chemicals talking. You soon find yourself becoming a different person within that relationship, and I don't mean in a good way either. It's called losing yourself, losing your purpose. As a result, you feel unfocused, get sick more, and feel like you are just going through the motions of life. Again, it all comes down to how much you value yourself. I know when I am working with a client if she's not valuing herself by simply looking at where her chaos resides.

The great news is that you can break out of the destructive pattern you are trapped in, that's ruining your relationships, financial situation, career, or spiritual path. The more you see that you matter, the easier it is to be in alignment with your life and attract what you want. If you see yourself as a high-value woman, you will keep moving in that direction.

I once worked with a very high-powered woman—one of the sharpest women I know—who found out her husband had cheated on her. She felt helpless, as if he was the only man on the planet. What was interesting to me was that she wanted to stay with him, despite his numerous affairs and the fact that he obviously wanted to end the relationship. He would tell her that he wanted them to stay together, but his personal values demonstrated otherwise. I revealed to her that because she wasn't valuing herself, she was trapped feeling hopeless; but it didn't have to be that way. She could become a high-value woman who could receive a man who would love her exactly the way she wanted, and in the context of a more balanced relationship. So I started having her get clear on her vision, just like we did in Chapter 6, so that she could learn to value herself and be able to receive.

**Fearless and Fabulous Female Profile**

**Anna Maria Tarantola** (born 1945) is famous for having launched a crusade against the excesses of television during the Silvio Berlusconi era, which, according to her, over-emphasized silicon-enhanced beauty and "vulgarity." She fought for more accurate, sophisticated representations of women, more in line with what Italian women actually are: people with character, skills, and talent.

I love learning about powerful women like Anna Maria, who are raising the standards of how women are viewed. I believe as women we must stand firm in who we are, confident in our power. Stop settling in your life and focus on what you truly desire. Pursue your passions, like Anna Maria has, and stay on your path.

She took the exercises seriously—and keep in mind that she had strong beliefs to overcome, because she was older, had been married twice, and thought that no one would want to date her. I told her that was complete crap, because I know that when you change your self-image, your outer world will shift. As soon as she reformulated her thinking, she quickly attracted a guy who was much more in alignment with her—just as I had promised. Stories like this are why I'm so inspired to do this work. There are so many fabulous women out there who I want to transform. Every day, I'm grateful for women like you, who are reading this book and want to change. They are ready to follow the La Dolce Vita Formula and live a life that is beyond whatever they previously imagined. You are not alone on this journey. Know that every day my vision is to inspire you to go after what you want.

*"Vivi la vita senza rimpianti."*
*("Live life with no regrets.")*

## Chapter Summary

The final piece to the La Dolce Vita Formula is to express gratitude on a regular basis. This chapter taught you how to create your Gratitude Formula, which is designed to rejuvenate you on a daily basis and keep you appreciating the many good things in your life, even if you are sailing challenging waters. Don't focus on what you are missing; find inspiration in all you have right now, as well as what is on the horizon.

# CHAPTER NINE
# SUMMARY AND NEXT STEPS

My hope is that after reading this book, you feel fully equipped and inspired to follow your own La Dolce Vita Formula and achieve your goals. If you've rigorously done the exercises laid out in the previous chapters, you have identified what your personal values are, and your actions are in alignment with your true goals and desires. You are now ready to wow the world and take your life to the next level! You are in the flow. There will certainly be obstacles along the way, but you've learned techniques and tactics to confront and surpass the challenges life throws your way.

One of the most important things I've discussed in this book is changing your mental state. Your unconscious mind is responsible for 95 percent of your beliefs, habits, and behaviors, and knowing how to rewire your mind is the secret to achieving your goals. It gives you the confidence to feel unstoppable because you have the tools to benefit from anything that comes your way. Taking action is of course another critical part of the achievement equation, and in some ways is the entire point of the book—learning how to take actions that are aligned with who you are and what you want inevitably leads to success. When you marry that with daily use of your Gratitude Formula, you find yourself powerfully inspired to shape and create your destiny.

It's my mission to help women empower all seven areas of their lives. I'm inspired to do this because, as I've related, in the past I was disempowered in many areas of my life. But after discovering my personal La Dolce Vita Formula, I've been able to transform my health and now love my body when once I hated it. I've shed excess pounds and have kept them off. I don't let age define me; rather I create new rules for being timeless and ageless. I've left my hopeless relationships behind and have now found my soul mate in a conscientious, loving man. He's my complementary opposite, and we help each other to walk our respective spiritual paths.

I've learned to be more masterful in my communications, both in the personal space and the business world. I've let go of worrying about money and have learned how to create valuable services and products worldwide that are making a real difference for women. I have a vast vision of helping millions of women this way, a vision that has started to come true. I am on the right spiritual path, pursuing my dreams, living my La Dolce Vita Formula.

I mention my life not to boast, but to show you that you and I are similar, and that if I could overcome the obstacles in my way, you can, too. Don't let anyone or anything stop you. You can be fabulous, fearless, and live a fulfilling life. Just make the decision every day to take action. And never stop working on your mind—everything else will follow.

"The strongest action for a woman is love herself, follow her truth, and live fabulously."

### What Are Your Next Steps?

Now that you have the formula to achieve your La Dolce Vita dreams, you're clear on what you want, and you have the tools and techniques to get out of your own way, then the next step I recommend is to plan out your La Dolce Vita Goals. To do this, first go back and read the La Dolce Vita Vision Statement you wrote, which defines what you want to accomplish, who you want to be, and what you want to have for the rest of your life. Then pick your most inspiring 1–3 goals you want to work on right now. Break them down into 30-, 60-, and 90-day subgoals. I find that breaking your goals into chunks like this simplifies the entire process and better focuses your mind on taking daily, inspired action steps.

Now that you've got your goals identified and broken down into doable chunks, you'll also want to create what I call the La Dolce Vita Success Rituals, which is a list of daily actions, steps, and habits that make it easier for you to move forward every day and measure your progress. Think about the good habits and actions that you want to repeat, day in and day out, and write them down. Also indicate *when* you want to do these things: in the morning, afternoon, evening. When finished, your La Dolce Vita Success Rituals list will serve as a handy tool to inspire you with all the good things you have to look forward to each day, not to mention making planning your schedule that much easier. All the important things are already in place!

Stay focused, get accountable, and masterfully plan each day to reach your dreams. If you think you need help on this front, check out the tools I've developed, listed in the next section of the book, where I've also provides ways to stay in touch with me. In the meanwhile, never stop working on being the woman I know you can be, and never stop reaching for the stars!

**"Here's to La Dolce Vita!"**

# More information on The La Dolce Vita Formula

**Live Your La Dolce Vita Life in 30 Days Formula**

Get the system that goes with the book! I've created an online program called the **Live Your La Dolce Vita Life in 30 Days Formula**. This system, along with its accompanying physical journal, **The La Dolce Vita Planner**, is the perfect companion to get the most of the book. The online program and journal make it easy for you to record your goals and track your progress, and help you with the process of reprograming your mindset. Together, the book, online program, and journal synchronize to give you all the tools and strategies you need to go out and grab **Your Fabulous Life**.

**Learn more about the Live Your La Dolce Vita Life in 30 Days Formula at**

**www.LaDolceVitaFormula.com**

---

Did you remember to download your FREE La Dolce Vita Vision worksheet that we mentioned at the beginning of the book? You'll need it for the vision statement exercise in Chapter 6. Here's the link:

**www.FearlessandFabulousVision.com**

## Stay in touch with the La Dolce Vita Formula community!

**Looking for personal coaching or consulting?**
I'm available for private coaching and consulting, so feel free to reach out to me at **www.SessionWithHeather.com** or by email at **support@heatherpicken.com**.

You can also visit **www.HeatherPicken.com** to get access to free training, articles, and other goodies.

**The La Dolce Vita Show**
Check out my show, **La Dolce Vita: The Formula For Fabulous Living**. Topics include mindset, breaking through limitations, and action steps you can take to get to the next level of your life. Go to ITunes and search for my show.

**Social Media**
Blog and main site: **www.HeatherPicken.com**
Instagram: **@heatherpicken**
Twitter: **@heatherpicken**
YouTube: **https://www.youtube.com/heatherpicken**
Facebook: **HeatherPickenLDV**

**Speaking and Media Appearances**
Hire me to speak at your organization, school, corporate training seminar, or leadership workshop. I also frequently appear on TV, radio, and podcast interviews.

**Specialized Training**
Demartini Institute: Values Determination Training
Facilitator of The Demartini Method®
Certified Hypnotherapist, Parrillo Certified Health and Fitness Trainer

## A Request to My Readers

My mission is to help as many women as possible achieve their goals and live fabulous, fulfillling lives. But to do that, I need your help to spread the word. If you found *The La Dolce Vita Formula* to be just what you needed to inspire you to be all you can be, I would be grateful if you would go to Amazon.com and give this book a 5-star rating and write a short review.

I know I can't please everyone, and I've thought long and hard about what I wanted to include in this book (and what I didn't) in order for you, my fabulous reader, to get results. If you have any feedback to share with me, positive or critical, please email me at **support@heatherpicken.com**. I am always thrilled to hear from people like you!

# Recommended Reading

If you enjoy books like *The La Dolce Vita Formula*, here's my Top 10 list for further reading. Each of these books has been a source of inspiration for me:

*You Can Heal Your Life*, by Louise L. Hay

*The Biology of Belief: Unleashing the Power of Consciousness, Matter & Miracles*, by Bruce H. Lipton

*You Are the Placebo: Making Your Mind Matter*, by Dr. Joe Dispenza

*Think and Grow Rich*, by Napoleon Hill

*Psycho-Cybernetics*, by Maxwell Maltz

*The Power of Your Subconscious Mind: Unlock the Secrets Within*, by Joseph Murphy

*Big Magic: Creative Living Beyond Fear*, by Elizabeth Gilbert

*The ONE Thing: The Surprisingly Simple Truth Behind Extraordinary Results*, by Gary Keller and Jay Papasan

*The Power of Intention: Learning to Co-create Your World Your Way*, by Wayne W. Dyer

*The Seven Spiritual Laws of Success: A Practical Guide to the Fulfillment of Your Dreams*, by Deepak Chopra

**"Your power will come from you owning it, from fully embracing yourself and what YOU believe"**

## About Heather Picken

Heather Picken is a renowned high-performance specialist and business coach, bestselling author, and television host. She empowers women to break through their limiting beliefs so they can achieve their personal and professional goals. Heather hosts the national television show *La Dolce Vita: The Formula for Fabulous Living*. She was inspired to create *The La Dolce Vita Formula* while living abroad in Italy, where her observations of Italian culture revealed secrets to achieving health, wealth, and success in all areas of life.

For more information, visit: **www.HeatherPicken.com**